CONTENTS

Introduction   4

When to visit.. 5
What's new 6
Isle of Wight at a glance 8
Things not to miss.. 10
Itineraries.. 18

Places   25

Cowes and around.. 26
Newport and around..................................... 36
Ryde and around... 44
The east coast 50
The south coast.. 56
Ventnor to Blackgang 64
Brighstone to Alum Bay 74
Yarmouth and around.................................... 82
Further afield 90

Accommodation   101

Essentials   109

Arrival 110
Getting around 111
Directory A–Z 114
Festivals and events 118
Chronology.. 119
Small print and index.................................. 121

T0017981

ISLE OF WIGHT

The Isle of Wight lies a short distance from the south coast of England, and spans just 23 miles at its widest point. This charming spot is often seen as being anchored in the past; you only have to visit the likes of Shanklin's thatched cottages or Godshill's quaint tearooms to experience this for yourself. Yet there's a liveliness that roars through the wind and over the headland with its bracing clifftop trails, exhilarating sailing scene and well-signposted cycling routes. Needless to say it's an idyllic spot for scenic strolls and harder hikes, with an absence of motorways on the island. Throw in a clutch of independent shops, stellar dining and almost always a room with a view, and you can see why so many want to make the most of this diamond-shaped island.

Stone houses on Winkle Street, Calbourne

The island has always been a popular holiday spot: Queen Victoria made Osborne House her permanent residence after her beloved consort Albert died, the Romantic poet Lord Tennyson enjoyed strolling across the downs near Freshwater, Charles Dickens also visited, and that's only rounding off the nineteenth century; in more recent years, Benedict Cumberbatch married in Mottistone and Kate Moss celebrated her hen-do in St Lawrence. The Isle of Wight is an inviting destination for 'mainlanders' (those visiting from mainland England) and further afield, drawn in by the island's beaches, which range from popular Ryde on the north coast to Compton Bay on the south coast, and plenty more sprinkled in between. Freshwater and Alum Bay on the west coast is home to the Needles, whose stunning landscape makes it a must-see on anyone's itinerary.

That said, the Isle of Wight is more than simply a bucket-and-spade destination. There's an abundance of history to take in, and in some parts it feels like not much has changed at all. You can appreciate this at numerous heritage centres across the island or see it first-hand for yourself at the likes of Yarmouth Castle, Old St Boniface Church and Bembridge Windmill. Chatting with

Freshwater Bay

the islanders (or 'nammets' as they call themselves, an old slang word used to describe a snack to eat when working in the fields) is another way to learn about the island's fascinating history on a local level, from tiger cub walks along Sandown beach to that Isle of Wight Festival and countless childhood stories retold at local museums.

Of course, seafood features on many a menu, with offerings of fresh Bembridge crab scrawled across blackboards outside cafés

When to visit

The Isle of Wight, along with the rest of the south of England, generally sees more hours of sunshine than the rest of the country. The island enjoys a relatively mild climate all year round but the summer period (May to September) is generally regarded as the best time to visit. This high season is when the island is at its liveliest, with the majority of the island's big-hitter festivals and events taking place. The cooler autumn months are a better bet for longer walks, cycles or hikes. A number of attractions close for the winter season but don't be put off, as there are fewer tourists, more accommodation options (usually at lower rates) and plenty of cosy pubs for you to warm up in. Spring is a great time to visit, with nature and wildlife at its best. Note that school holidays are popular times for escapes to the island – as well as the most expensive.

Yarmouth marina

and various fish caught locally and freshly cooked. You can eat out well on the Isle of Wight, with the majority of places very reasonably priced. Equally, if you want to splash the cash, there's no shortage of slick restaurants with menus as exclusive as the views.

The island is also one of the best places in Europe for dinosaur discoveries; in June 2022, the remains of Europe's largest ever land-based predator dinosaur were discovered here. Fossils date as far back as 136 million years ago – head to Compton Bay and at low tide you can spot dinosaur footprints. There are many informative tours and walks led by experts, so you can suss out your flint from your fossils.

Even if the weather isn't on your side, there are plenty of non-weather-reliant things to do: there's a zoo, numerous museums, a dinosaur theme park and a steam railway to name a few. National Trust and English Heritage sites are well represented across the island – from Osborne House to Newtown Old Town Hall – and you should also make time to visit the chocolate-box towns of Brighstone, Yarmouth and Godshill. Many people visit the Isle of Wight as a day-trip from the mainland, but to really do it justice, give yourself at least a weekend (or ideally a week) to make the most of this underrated island. We promise you won't regret it.

What's new

Although Blackgang Chine's much-loved Cliffhanger rollercoaster took its final spin in October 2022, the UK's oldest theme park welcomed a brand-new ride, **Extinction**, in March 2023. The pendulum swing reaches hair-rising heights of 18m and completes full 360-degree spins – sending riders upside down – and is the largest of the park's rides. From the top, you'll be able to glimpse the lovely seaview, but you won't be hanging around for long before swooping back towards ground level...

Where to...

Shop

The majority of the island's shops are independent or family-based. There are weekly markets and delicatessens, small boutiques and a few high-street friendlies. Cowes caters to a large sailing crowd, so you'll find specialist stockists such as Musto, Henri Lloyd and Regatta, while Newport offers more mainstream shops. Ventnor is undergoing something of a quirky revolution with its vinyl record shops, vintage clothing boutiques and retro-culture stores, and some shops sell purely island-made products, which is a great way to showcase how much the island has to offer. Wine, gin, cheese, mustard, passata, garlic... the list goes on.

OUR FAVOURITES: Reggie's Retro, see page 70. The Velvet Pig, see page 48. Medina Books see page 32.

Eat

It goes without saying that the island's main cuisine is fish and seafood. From seabass and sole to monkfish and mullet, many restaurants pride themselves on sourcing the local catch and cooking it fresh. It's well worth feasting on much of the island's own produce, which can be enjoyed as part of a picnic or an item to take away. Expect a smattering of international cuisine – Thai, French, Italian – and an increasing range of veggie- and vegan dishes. Otherwise, you can't go wrong with the pub classics, from beer-battered cod to island-steak pies.

OUR FAVOURITES: Ristorante Michelangelo, see page 49. True Food Kitchen, see page 71. The Smoking Lobster, see page 70.

Drink

There are lots of pubs dotted around the island; cosy fisherman-types that make for perfect stops at the end of a long, windy walk or to take in the breathtaking coast and Solent views. Plus, be sure to visit Island Roasted Coffee, Goddard's Brewery and the Isle of Wight Distillery, where some of the best island produce is made. You can visit the majority of these as part of a tour with tastings, or simply purchase their products from various shops or order from coffee shops, pubs and restaurants alike.

OUR FAVOURITES: Isle of Wight Distillery, see page 51. Caffè Isola, see page 42. The Garlic Farm, see page 39.

Go out

Nightlife will never be what the island is famed for: bars and nightclubs are few, but what the Isle of Wight lacks here, it makes up for in abundance with its pubs. This is arguably the best way to get under the surface of Isle of Wight culture, with the island well-renowned for its variety of fantastic live music. This may be where you'll find many of the locals; in fact, some evenings you could stroll along a silent high street until you pass a small cove of a pub where all the noise – and people – are contained.

OUR FAVOURITES: The Anchor, see page 35. The Sun Inn, see page 81. The Spyglass Inn, see page 70.

Isle of Wight at a glance

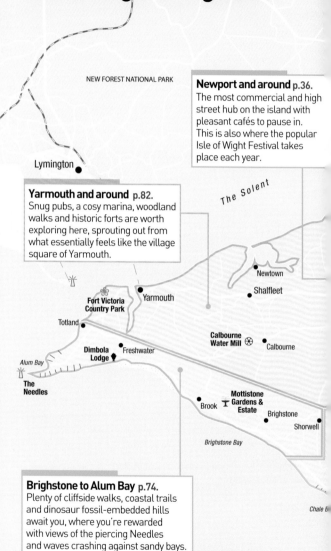

Newport and around p.36.
The most commercial and high street hub on the island with pleasant cafés to pause in. This is also where the popular Isle of Wight Festival takes place each year.

Yarmouth and around p.82.
Snug pubs, a cosy marina, woodland walks and historic forts are worth exploring here, sprouting out from what essentially feels like the village square of Yarmouth.

NEW FOREST NATIONAL PARK

Lymington

The Solent

Newtown

Shalfleet

Fort Victoria
Country Park

Yarmouth

Totland

Calbourne
Water Mill

Calbourne

Dimbola
Lodge

Freshwater

Alum Bay

The
Needles

Mottistone
Gardens &
Estate

Brook

Brighstone

Shorwell

Brighstone Bay

Chale B

Brighstone to Alum Bay p.74.
Plenty of cliffside walks, coastal trails and dinosaur fossil-embedded hills await you, where you're rewarded with views of the piercing Needles and waves crashing against sandy bays.

Ventnor to Blackgang p.64.
Vintage tearooms, long-sweeping vistas of the English Channel and an arty, independent edge to enjoy here, all within its own microclimate.

Cowes and around p.26.
This historic yachting town is filled with fashionable boutiques, high-end dining and is the site of the historic Cowes Week and other sailing events.

Ryde and around p.44.
A no-frills seaside stop, perfect for spending days on the beach, filled with fun activities for the kids and splendid views across to Portsmouth on the mainland.

The east coast p.50.
This quiet spot has lovely walks along the Duver, a range of upmarket properties to gawk at and independent shops worth a browse.

Portsmouth

The Solent

East Cowes

owes

wood

River Medina

Osborne House

Fishbourne

Quarr Abbey

Ryde

Wootton

Binstead

Seaview

Havenstreet

St Helens

Newport

Roman Villa

Carisbrooke
brooke
stle

Robin Hill Country Park

Nunwell House

The Garlic Farm

Brading Roman Villa

Brading

Bembridge Windmill

Blackwater

Wildheart Animal Sanctuary

combe

Rookley

Dinosaur Isle

Sandown

Amazon World

Godshill

Shanklin

Isle of Wight Donkey Sanctuary

Appuldurcombe House

Wroxall

Bonchurch

hale

St Catherine's Oratory

Botanical Gardens

Ventnor

ckgang
Chine

Niton

St Lawrence

ENGLISH CHANNEL

The south coast p.56.
Variety of landscapes from the depths of the Chine to the long stretches of beaches, complete with an old-world feel of thatched villages and traditional sweet shops.

15

Things not to miss

It's not possible to see everything the Isle of Wight has to offer in one trip – and we don't suggest you try. What follows is a selective taste of the island's highlights, from quaint pubs and intriguing, historic architecture to family-fun activities and bracing, windswept walks.

> The Garlic Farm
See page 39
Spend a morning learning all about garlic (yes, really) by going on a farm tour, before rewarding yourself with a scoop of garlic ice cream afterwards.

< Osborne House
See page 29
Queen Victoria and Prince Albert's family home, an Italianate Renaissance-style villa that makes for a fun day out.

∨ Robin Hill Country Park
See page 39
Tackle a treetop trail, wiggle down a toboggan ride and be wowed at the falconry displays in the 88 acres of woods here.

< **Bonchurch**
See page 67
Delightful village of thatched cottages and Victorian villas, once popular with many Victorian literary icons including Dickens and Keats.

∨ **The Needles**
See page 78
Take the chairlift down from the clifftop over Alum Bay to take in the island's iconic landmark in all its brilliant-white glory.

< **Brading Roman Villa**
See page 52

This impressive villa features incredible mosaics set in a modern museum, where you can learn all about British Roman life during the fourth century AD.

∨ **Blackgang Chine**
See page 69

The UK's oldest amusement park launched a brand-new ride in 2023. Perched on the clifftop, this attraction is an island rite of passage.

∧ **Tennyson Down**
See page 76
Beautiful stretch of rolling downs that can be enjoyed as part of a long or shorter walk, and pause by the Tennyson Monument at the top.

< **Isle of Wight Distillery**
See page 51
Sip a Mermaid Gin and tonic while listening to an informal talk about the island's own gin distillery at this laidback pub-bar.

∧ Shanklin Old Village
See page 59
Pink-washed pubs, low thatched cottages, homely pubs with Old English charm... there's no denying that Shanklin is one of the quaintest spots on the island.

∨ St Catherine's Point
See page 69
With its standout lighthouse and medieval tower, there's plenty of maritime history to take in here, plus scenic coastal walks.

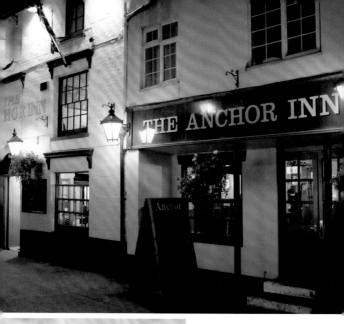

∧ **The Anchor Inn**
See page 35
Head to this premier live music spot on the island on a Wednesday, Friday or Saturday night for a fun evening of fab jazz, rock or blues.

< **Steam Railway**
See page 40
All aboard this heritage railway, which rolls through five miles of picturesque countryside from Wootton Common to Smallbrook Junction in Ryde.

< **Yarmouth Castle**
See page 83
Once the island's main port, the castle was King Henry VIII's last coastal defence and today boasts superb views over the estuary.

∨ **Coastal walks**
See page 22
There are plenty of coastal trails to enjoy at any time of the year which wrap around various parts of the island with unique vistas.

THINGS NOT TO MISS

Day one on the Isle of Wight

Morning wake-up call. See page 34. Start the day at an inviting café like *Eegon's of Cowes* and stock up on homemade treats like cakes, sausage rolls and pasties.

Osborne House. See page 29. Spend the best part of the morning exploring the grounds here, which include landscaped gardens, staterooms, a beach and the Swiss Cottage.

Lunch. See page 42. Take the bus outside Osborne House to Newport, and stop for a baguette and a slice of cake at *The Blue Door*.

Carisbrooke Castle. See page 37. This Norman keep now houses a museum, Edwardian-style gardens and 16th-century well-house, as well as resident donkeys.

The Garlic Farm. See page 39. Venture a little outside of Newport and explore the farm on a tractor tour, then buy everything garlic-related at their on-site shop.

Dinner. See page 34. Sample one of Cowes' best restaurants at *The Smoking Lobster*, with an Asian-infused menu including katsu fish of the day.

Real ale. See page 35. Directly opposite the restaurant is *The Anchor Inn*, which is perfect for a nightcap, or take a post-dinner stroll to *The Vectis Tavern*.

Osbourne House

Carisbrooke Castle

Garlic Farm

Day two on the Isle of Wight

Yarmouth Pier. See page 83. Start the day with a walk along this Victorian, Grade II-listed pier and keep an eye out for shy porpoises.

The Needles. See page 78. Hike along the cliff tops to marvel at the three chalk stacks that once connected the island to the mainland.

Old & New Battery. See page 78. Continue round to take in Victorian coastal defence fort, underground rooms and original cannon guns.

Lunch. Tuck into island-sourced grub on one of the picnic tables or spread out a blanket on the grass.

Tennyson Down. See page 76. Follow the trail along to Freshwater Bay, a popular 7-mile walk that can also be split into two shorter walks.

Dimbola Lodge. See page 76. Warm up with a hot drink in the tearoom before wandering through the rooms showcasing Victorian photographer Julia Margaret Cameron's work.

Dinner. See page 89. *The Bugle Inn* serves well-earned pub grub in a stylish setting, and if the weather's nice, enjoy a sundowner outside on the terrace.

Yarmouth Pier

The Needles

Dimbola Lodge

Family island

The island is a perfect destination for families and groups, and there's plenty of self-catering accommodation; below are recommended activities and sights worth checking out.

Ryde. See page 44. Kids can frolic on the beach, go wild at the funfair or even go tree-climbing. There's plenty of beachfront eating spots to wind down (or get through) the day with.

Blackgang Chine. See page 69. Entertaining theme park in a great location; most of the rides are suitable for under-12s.

West Wight Alpacas. See page 83. Spend the day visiting alpacas, llamas, rabbits and more at this farm near Yarmouth, where kids can also feed the lambs.

Wildheart Animal Sanctuary. See page 57. Watch the keepers feed the animals, listen to an informative talk and check out the well-cared-for Big Cats, monkeys and reptiles.

Dinosaur Isle. See page 59. Learn all about the island's fascinating dinosaur history with life-sized replicas and informative displays, and get hands on with a guided fossil walk – who knows what you might discover?

Robin Hill Country Park. See page 39. Loads of themed play areas that are well-suited to various age groups; activities include zip wires, a maze and falconry displays.

Ryde seafront

Wildheart Animal Sanctuary

Dinosaur Isle

Budget island

Swap fine-dining for picnics and fancy hotels for campgrounds and caravan parks. It's easy enough to make the most of the island without splashing the cash!

Heritage Centres. See pages 28 and 65. There are heritage centres dotted all over the island. As they are free to visit and largely reliant on volunteers, you might want to make a small donation.

Donkey Sanctuary. See page 68. With over a hundred donkeys and ponies, this sanctuary provides great care for the animals – and it's free to visit, although donations are always welcome.

Campsites. See page 102. One of the most popular (and affordable) ways to stay on the Isle of Wight, with campsites and holiday caravan parks dotted across the island.

Coastal walks. Enjoy routes from Colwell to Totland (see page 75), Ryde to Seaview (see page 50) or along Ventnor Esplanade (see page 64). Round it off with a cone of chips or ice cream on the beach.

Picnics. Do your bit for the local community and stock up on local produce for when you're halfway across the headlands and there's not a café in sight.

Steam Railway. See page 40. A full-day unlimited ticket sees you explore the pretty countryside, themed train stations and yesteryear feel of the rolling landscape.

Donkey Sanctuary

Coastal walk

Steam railway trip

Walking the island

The Isle of Wight is one of the most popular destinations for walkers across the country, with well-signposted coastal routes providing amazing views in almost every direction.

Cowes to Yarmouth: Start your route in West Cowes along Medina Road; after Thorness Bay you'll wind slightly further inland to Locksgreen and Shalfleet before returning to the coast at Hamsted. The trail leads onto Yarmouth, where this route ends. This is a 16-mile (26km) gentle route with slight inclines.

Yarmouth to Brighstone: This route winds you past The Needles, the island's most iconic sight, in all its ridged-chalk glory. Once you turn the corner, the English Channel will swing into view – you're now on the south of the island – before finishing up at Brighstone Village. This is a 14-mile (23km) route with steep sections.

Sandown to Ryde: This route takes in the bucket-and-spade favourites on the island, starting at Sandown Pier, around to Bembridge Harbour and up through plush Seaview before Portsmouth on the mainland swings into view and it's straight on to Ryde. This is a 12-mile (19km) trail that is a fairly gentle route.

Ryde to East Cowes: For the most historic walk, pick this one, which sees you take in abbey ruins, Osbourne House and the Royal Yacht Squadron, one of the oldest sailing clubs in the world. Starting at lively Ryde, you'll travel a little inland to cross over Wootton Bridge, before passing by Whippingham – near Osborne House – and reaching East Cowes. This is a 8-mile (13km) walk that is an easy route with gentle slopes.

Coastal path near Compton Bay

Woodland path near Sandown

Cowes Floating Bridge

Rainy day island

You don't have to time your visit with the summer months. Covering castles, museums and theatres, here's how to make the best of a rainy or chillier day on the island.

Osborne House. See page 29. While away the best part of a morning exploring the spectacular interiors of Queen Victoria's family home, which include the Indian-decorated Durbar Room, exotic hothouses, nursery rooms and royal bathrooms.

🍴 **Time for tea.** From spacious coffee shops to twee tearooms, there are plenty of places worth stopping off at for afternoon tea, a slice of cake or island-roasted coffee. Get your caffeine fix at Newport's *Caffe Isola* (see page 42) or don your best floral print in Shanklin's *Old Thatch Tearoom* (see page 63).

Shanklin Theatre. See page 59. Year-round productions are held in this Victorian-age theatre, just back from the high street and a 10min walk from the Old Village. There's something for everyone here, from backstage tours to comedy nights with the likes of Sarah Millican, and wilderness tales with Ben Fogle, amongst others.

Isle of Wight Distillery See page 51. Decorated with repurposed Mermaid Gin bottles, this cosy bar gives you space to chat with locals and other visitors, learn the site's gin-distilling process and generally not make plans to leave any time soon.

Brading Roman Villa. See page 52. This award-winning museum provides a detailed insight into life in Roman Britain; check out the mosaic floors, well-preserved archaeology and designated craft areas, breathing life into a time long-gone.

The Durbar Room at Osborne House

Shanklin Theatre

Brading Roman Villa

PLACES

Cowes and around......................................**26**

Newport and around **36**

Ryde and around **44**

The east coast **50**

The south coast **56**

Ventnor to Blackgang **64**

Brighstone to Alum Bay **74**

Yarmouth and around **82**

Further afield..**90**

The Isle of Wight's beautiful coastline

Cowes and around

Situated at the northern tip of the Isle of Wight and close to the mainland, Cowes is the first port of call for most visitors. This little town is bisected by the River Medina, with lively West Cowes connected to sleepy East Cowes by a floating chain bridge. West Cowes is a haven for yachties while East Cowes is home to Osborne House (Queen Victoria's holiday home and later permanent residence), which is arguably the biggest tourist attraction on the entire island. West Cowes is one of the most upmarket areas, its narrow streets laden with boutique shops, historic pubs and smart restaurants. The town is inextricably associated with sailing craft and boat building: in 1826, the first Cowes Week commenced here and today it's one of the busiest times of the calendar year.

The Sir Max Aitken Museum

MAP P.30
83 High St, PO31 7AJ. http://
sirmaxaitkenmuseum.org. Free.
Named after a keen yachtsman who
(successfully) represented Great

Britain at sailing events, a visit to
the small **Max Aitken Museum**
is a decent way to learn about the
town's maritime history. Set along
the high street in an eighteenth-
century sailmaker's loft, the
museum contains a whole host of

The Sir Max Aitken Museum

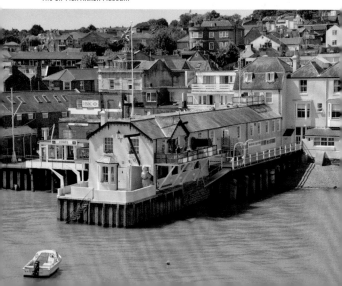

Classic Boat Museum

maritime paraphernalia: model boats, figureheads, artefacts from royal yachts and more.

Cowes Maritime Museum

MAP P.30

Beckford Road. 01983 823433. Free.
Situated in one large room at the back of Cowes Library, the little **Cowes Maritime Museum** charts the town's sailing and boatbuilding history with a selection of interesting marine and sailing photography, as well as sailing objects and boatbuilding plans. There's also a dress-up box and colouring table for the kids.

Classic Boat Museum

MAP P.30

Albany Rd, PO32 6AA. http://
classicboatmuseum.org. Charge.
The **Classic Boat Museum** is set across two sites: the **Gallery** in East Cowes and the **Boat Shed** in West Cowes. The Boat Shed has nearly 90 different boats on display, as well as the restored optic from St Catherine's Lighthouse, while the Gallery displays more boating memorabilia, which includes

various photography collections. There's an abundance of items on display here, with informative boards about significant figures in the boating world, from Joe Carstairs, an eccentric 1920s powerboat racer memorialised as 'the fastest woman on water' to local girl Dame Ellen MacArthur, who broke the world record for the fastest solo circumnavigation of the world in 2005.

The Parade

MAP P.30

One of the island's many coastal walks, the route along the **Parade** to Egypt Point features a couple of noteworthy historic points. Starting on Victoria Esplanade at the RNLI Lifeboat Station, you'll pass the Royal Yacht Squadron on your left, once one of Henry VIII's castles and now home to perhaps the most prestigious sailing club in the world, used as a starting point for many sailing races today. This curves onto Queen's Parade, along a short shingle beach and past an otherwise unassuming white cottage, Rosetta Cottage. The plaque on the pavement opposite explains that this was where Lord Randolph Churchill first met and proposed to a Jennie Jerome in 1873; their first son was born in 1874. His name? Winston Churchill. The vista-filled walk ends a little further up at Egypt Point.

Northwood Park

MAP P.28

Northwood House & Park, Ward Avenue, PO31 8AZ. www.northwoodhouse.org. Free.

The 17-acre **Northwood Park** is a perfect spot for walks, picnics or even a game of tennis or bowls (courts are free to use). The Grade II-listed House holds private functions, so you can't go inside, but you can still enjoy the neoclassical exterior, with its palladium front and columns. There are lots of different types of trees here, the majority planted before the nineteenth century,

including one supposedly gifted from Queen Victoria herself. Its position on the hill lends itself to some fine clear sea views.

East Cowes Heritage Centre

MAP P.30

8 Clarence Road, PO32 6EP. www. eastcowesheritage.co.uk. Free, donations appreciated.

Essentially a one-shop floor that's been converted into a display room, the **Heritage Centre** displays permanent exhibitions of East Cowes' history since 1783. There's an in-depth display about Queen Victoria's fondness of the area – particularly Norris House, where she summered when she was younger (and was the inspiration for Osborne House). It's worth a visit if just to get a background on Osborne House, before you take the trek (or bus) uphill afterwards.

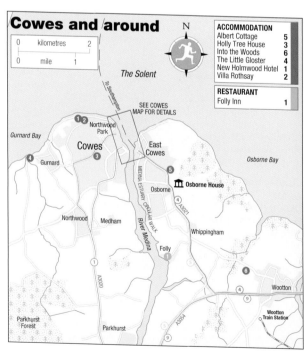

Cowes and around

N

ACCOMMODATION	
Albert Cottage	5
Holly Tree House	3
Into the Woods	6
The Little Gloster	4
New Holmwood Hotel	1
Villa Rothsay	2

RESTAURANT	
Folly Inn	1

The Solent

SEE COWES MAP FOR DETAILS

To Southampton

Gurnard Bay

Northwood Park

Cowes

Gurnard

East Cowes

Osborne Bay

Osborne House

Osborne

Northwood

Medham

River Medina

MEDINA ESTUARY CIRCULAR WALK

Whippingham

Folly

Wootton

Wootton Train Station

Parkhurst Forest

Parkhurst

Gardens at Osborne House

Osborne House

MAP P.28
York Ave, PO32 6JX. Bus #4 to Ryde or #5 to Newport from East Cowes. www.english-heritage.org.uk/visit/places/Osborne. Charge.

Here's a little-known fact: the young, pre-queen Victoria used to spend her summers at nearby Norris Castle, but later on, the owner would not sell it to Albert. Undeterred, Albert built Osborne House with the help of Thomas Cubitt in the late 1840s, and it became the royal family's holiday home. Styled as an Italianate villa with honey-coloured balconies and expansive terraces, it overlooks sprawling landscaped gardens and on towards the Solent. Today, it's an English Heritage site that is a must-see while on the Isle of Wight. Although this was Queen Victoria's holiday home, the staterooms are still quite formal, but the private apartments retain a homely feel. Following Albert's death in 1861, Queen Victoria moved into Osborne House until her own death in 1901. The

Cowes Week

Early August sees the international yachting festival, Cowes Week (http://cowesweek.co.uk), which is the largest sailing regatta in the world. Up to 100,000 spectators watch around a thousand boats take part, commandeered by sailors of all abilities – including enthusiastic amateurs, royalty and Olympic champions. The race first took place in 1826 (with just seven yachts) and has occurred every year since except during the world wars and at the height of the coronavirus pandemic in 2020. Throughout the festival there's a great party atmosphere and dozens of organized events, including a spectacular firework display on the final Friday night. In addition to Cowes Week, most summer weekends see some form of nautical event taking place in or around town.

Note that rates for accommodation almost double during Cowes Week, when places need to be booked months ahead.

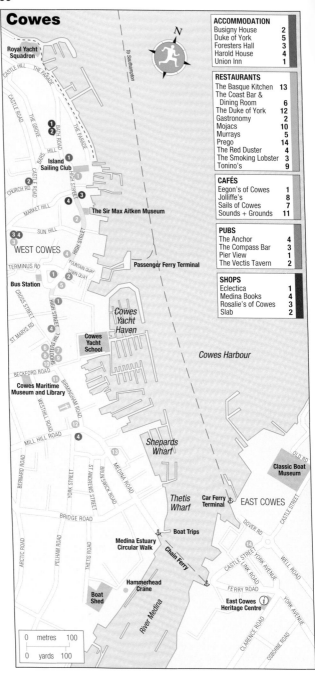

Cowes

ACCOMMODATION

Busigny House	2
Duke of York	5
Foresters Hall	3
Harold House	4
Union Inn	1

RESTAURANTS

The Basque Kitchen	13
The Coast Bar & Dining Room	6
The Duke of York	12
Gastronomy	2
Mojacs	10
Murrays	5
Prego	14
The Red Duster	4
The Smoking Lobster	3
Tonino's	9

CAFÉS

Eegon's of Cowes	1
Jolliffe's	8
Sails of Cowes	7
Sounds + Grounds	11

PUBS

The Anchor	4
The Compass Bar	3
Pier View	1
The Vectis Tavern	2

SHOPS

Eclectica	1
Medina Books	4
Rosalie's of Cowes	3
Slab	2

Royal Yacht Squadron

To Southampton

Island Sailing Club

The Sir Max Aitken Museum

WEST COWES

Passenger Ferry Terminal

Bus Station

Cowes Yacht Haven

Cowes Yacht School

Cowes Harbour

Cowes Maritime Museum and Library

Shepards Wharf

Classic Boat Museum

Thetis Wharf

Car Ferry Terminal

EAST COWES

Boat Trips

Medina Estuary Circular Walk

Chain Ferry

Hammerhead Crane

Boat Shed

East Cowes Heritage Centre

River Medina

| 0 | metres | 100 |
| 0 | yards | 100 |

The world's largest yacht race

The **Round the Island Race** is a two-day sailing event which first launched in 1931. It attracts competitors from far and wide, from the Channel Islands to the USA. Sailing yachts must circumnavigate the island: commencing at the Royal Yacht Squadron (where else?), the route heads westwards round The Needles and St Catherine's Point, on past Bembridge and then back to Cowes, taking four to five hours in all. To find out more, visit www.roundtheisland.org.uk.

house hasn't really changed too much since then, so this is a fantastic way to gain an intimate insight into royal family life. A fifteen-minute walk through the gardens leads onto Swiss Cottage, where Victoria and Albert's nine children made good use of this two-storey playhouse. Afterwards, head down to the private beach, where you can go for a dip or take a peek at the restored bathing machine, a green-panelled cart that would be wheeled into the sea for Victoria to change and step into the sea from.

Whippingham

MAP P.28

Whippingham is a small village just a mile south of Osborne House, leading on towards Newport; it was once part of the royal estate. It's one of those classic Isle of Wight villages where not much seems to have changed in the past few centuries: think winding country roads, vast green fields and the Royal Church of St Mildred. With its west side flanking the River Medina, you can either pause at the waterside *Folly Inn* (see page 33) or carry on down to the East Cowes Marina, and mooch along the public footpath while passing by sailing yachts and gleaming speedboats.

Medina Estuary Circular Walk

MAP P.28

This **nine-mile walk** is flat but long, stretching from the West Cowes floating bridge terminal all the way round to East Cowes. Follow the former railway line route to Newport (public footpath #29), cross the bridge at the marina's entrance and follow the signposts towards *The Folly Inn* at Whippingham. From here, you'll wind inland to East Cowes, from where you can board the floating bridge back to West Cowes. This route is part of the Round the Island Cycle Route and Isle of Wight Coastal Path.

Gurnard Bay

MAP P.28

Following on from Egypt Point leads immediately onto Prince's Esplanade, which brings you to the quiet village of Gurnard. The Bay is lined with a row of beach huts looking onto a shingle beach, and is a popular spot to discover the fossils of insects.

Royal Church of St Mildred

Shops

Eclectica

MAP P.30

14-15 Bath Rd, PO31 7QN. www.
eclecticacowes.co.uk.

Selling antiques, collectables and
retro finds, this store truly lives
up to its name. Here you'll find
one-of-a-kind items like Art Deco
mirrors, vintage vases and original
1970s Isle of Wight Festival
posters.

Medina Books

MAP P.30

50 High St, PO31 7RR. http://
medinabookshop.com.

This independent bookshop
supplies a range of paperback
and hardback books, covering
island-related titles (including this
one!), fiction, maritime history and
children's literature.

Rosalie's of Cowes

MAP P.30

74 High St, PO31 7AJ. https://
rosaliesofcowes.co.uk/.

Stock up on French flavours, from
jars of green olive tapenade to

guinea fowl terrine. Aside from
France's best pates, soups and jams,
you'll also find local island produce
by Isle of Wight Biscuits, The
Garlic Farm and more. Perfect for
picnics.

Slab

MAP P.30

13 Bath Road, PO31 7QN. http://slabfudge.
co.uk.

The husband-and-wife duo who
run Slab create artisan fudge on-site
in a range of flavours, from cherry
and lemon meringue to sea-salted
caramel and chocolate orange
(£3.50 each). Large vegan range
and zero-waste packaging.

Restaurants

The Basque Kitchen

MAP P. 30

Medina Rd, PO31 7HT. http://
thebasquekitchen.co.uk.

Close to the chain ferry, *The Basque
Kitchen* serves authentic cuisine
from the Basque region, and the
entire menu is gluten-free and
locally sourced. Tapas-wise, tuck
into txistorra (Basque chorizo) and

Slab Artisan Fudge

Galician-style octopus, or go all-out with their sharing one-kilogram steak, served with hand-cut chips and peppers. £

The Coast Bar & Dining Room

MAP P.30

15 Shooters Hill, West Cowes, PO31 7BG. http://thecoastbar.co.uk.

Popular bar-restaurant with a lively, sophisticated vibe. On the menu is curried butternut squash and sweet potato pie (£15) and wood-fired pizza (from £11.75). A great spot for an upmarket breakfast, lunch or dinner. ££

The Duke of York

MAP P.30

Mill Hill Rd, PO31 7BT. http://dukeofyorkcowes.co.uk.

Also a hotel, *The Duke of York* features a great deal of dishes, from pub classics (pies £13.50) and luxury crab cakes (£17.95) to halloumi burgers (£12.95) and traditional Sunday Roasts (£11.95). £

Folly Inn

MAP P.28

Folly Lane, Whippingham, PO32 6NB. https://www.greeneking-pubs.co.uk/pubs/isle-of-wight/folly/.

Set in the sleepy village of Whippingham, this waterside pub is a perfect stop-off after visiting Osborne House. While you tuck into decent grub (pies, fajitas and more in the £13–£20 range), the river licks the decks. There's also a gluten-free menu and for lighter bites, opt for one of their signature sandwiches (around £7). £

Gastronomy

MAP P.30

46 High Street, PO31 7BE. www.gastronomycowes.co.uk.

Slick interior and fine meals to match, with the likes of wild mushroom and chilli linguine (£16.50) and tacos (£9-11) on the

Local ale

menu. Or pop in for a cocktail – their happy hour covers two cocktails for £15. ££

Mojacs

MAP P.30

10a Shooters Hill, PO31 7BG. http://mojacs.co.uk.

Intimate restaurant serving up well-presented dishes at admirable prices, such as Isle of Wight fillet steak (£32) and brie- and bacon-stuffed chicken breast (£17.50). They also have an extensive gin, wine and cocktail menu. £££

Murrays

MAP P.30

106 High St, PO31 7AT. http://murrays.co.

Much-loved seafood restaurant close to the marina, particularly popular with yachting parties. They source local fish so the menu changes depending on the season, or you can opt for a set-price menu (two-course lunch £23.50, three-course dinner £31) or the catch of the day. £££

Prego

MAP P.30

28 Castle St, PO31 6RD. http://pregoiow.uk.

Tonino's

Whether you want to eat in or take away, this informal Italian restaurant-café serves brunch, lunch and dinner right by the Red Funnell port. Busy with locals and visitors alike, enjoy the spicy and non-spicy pizzas (£10-13) or spaghetti primavera (£13.50). £

The Red Duster
MAP P.30
37 High St, PO31 7RS. http://theredduster.com.

With a distinctive red exterior and six or so booths inside, there's a jovial atmosphere amongst staff and patrons alike here. Opt for citrus-grilled yellowfin sole (£19.95) or smoking-hot enchiladas (£16.50). £

The Smoking Lobster
MAP P.30
127 High St, PO31 7AY. https://www.smokinglobstercowes.co.uk.

Ideally situated between *The Anchor Inn* and Cowes Marina, this pan-Asian restaurant goes all-out with whole or half lobster (market price), ginger-baked seabass (£27) and a seafood platter for two (£90). If you've room for a boozy digestif, try the plum-infused sweet sake. ££

Tonino's
MAP P.30
8–9 Shooters Hill, PO31 7BE. www.toninoscowes.co.uk.

An inviting ambience and Puglian-inspired cuisine await you at this long-running, family-run Italian restaurant. The extensive menu of authentic pasta, pizza, meat and fish dishes makes choosing difficult, but we couldn't get enough of the monkfish stew (£20.95). ££

Cafés

Eegon's of Cowes
MAP P.30
72 High St, PO31 7RE. http://eegonsofcowes.weebly.com.

The best breakfast spot in Cowes, serving Full English's' (£6.50), veggie breakfasts (£7) and plenty of hearty lunch options from £5. Those feeling extra hungry can go for their larger breakfasts and, as the sign outside reads, Eegon's is perfect for hangovers. £

Jolliffe's
MAP P.30
11 Shooters Hill, PO31 7BE. https://www.facebook.com/jolliffeseatery.

Green-tiled Art Nouveau building serving hearty breakfasts, lunches, cream teas and hot drinks, with upstairs seating. The shoe display nods to the building's origins as a bootmaking business. £

Sails of Cowes

MAP P.30

1 Shooters Hill, PO31 7BE. https:// sailsofcowes.co.uk/.
Dinky café with indoor and outdoor seating, ideal for food and drink to take away too. Whether you're after pancakes, paninis, breakfast or baguettes, this simple, modern café doesn't disappoint. £

Sounds + Grounds

MAP P.30

12 Birmingham Road, PO31 7BH. https://www.facebook.com/ soundsandgroundsiow/.
Is this the coolest spot in Cowes? We certainly think so. This coffee shop stocks vinyl records from various genres – film soundtracks, Hip-Hop, Soul – and champions local talent with regular live music. £

Pubs

The Anchor Inn

MAP P.30

1–3 High St, PO31 7SA. www. theanchorcowes.co.uk.
The go-to spot for the island's best live music, with local and mainland bands covering all genres, from rock and jazz to indie and ska. There's a small 'dancefloor' space too. There's a choice of real ale, ciders, beers and wine, as well as standard pub grub, which you can enjoy in the beer garden or inside by the fireplace. £

The Compass Bar

MAP P.30

10 High St, PO31 7RZ. https://compassbar. co.uk/.

The Compass Bar pride themselves on their fab cocktail and wine list – and we can't fault it, either. Slick wooden flooring and bar with exposed brick walls and, come evening, pink lighting. It makes for a fun alternative from the string of pubs. £

Pier View

MAP P.30

25 High St, PO31 7RY. http:// pierviewcowes.co.uk.
This pub and kitchen is popular with yachties and is good for its proximity to the West Cowes ferry terminal. Although it's primarily a sports bar, they also run a weekly pub quiz and their menu covers burgers (from £14.50), mains (breaded scampi £14.50) and baguettes (£9). £

The Vectis Tavern

MAP P.30

103 High St, PO31 7AT. www.vectistavern. co.uk.
Established in 1757, this pub is still just as popular with the locals and retains real character. It has a beer garden and hosts quiz nights, live music and karaoke. £

Watch House Café

Newport and around

Newport, the island capital, sits at the centre of the island. Although its town centre bustles with high street activity, Watchbell Lane is a quaint little slice wedged in between the high street shops. Newport is best-known as the site of the Isle of Wight Festival (held at Seaclose Park). Yet venture slightly further out and you'll stumble across some of the island's top attractions, including Carisbrooke Castle, a Roman villa, Robin Hill Country Park and the start of the steam railway. Seeing as so many bus routes pass through Newport or require you to transfer buses here, you may as well see what the market town has to offer.

Museum of Island History

MAP P.38
High St, PO30 1TY. 01983 823433. Charge.

Designed by the renowned Regency/Georgian architect John Nash (of Buckingham Palace fame), the Guildhall previously served as

a market, fire station, banqueting hall and shop. Today it serves as the island's tourist office and the **Museum of Island History**. If you're fascinated by dinosaurs or simply want to find out more about the island's fascinating history with

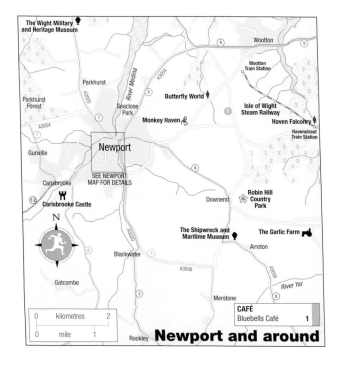

Newport and around

Monkey Haven

them, take in the array of fossils and dinosaur bones that have been discovered across the Isle of Wight. Dinosaurs aside, you can find out much more about the island's history with the likes of photographs, touch-screen displays and even Anglo-Saxon jewellery, swords and axes on display.

Monkey Haven

MAP P.36
Staplers Road, PO30 2NB. Bus #9 to Staplers Road bus stop. http://monkeyhaven.org. Charge.
The award-winning **Monkey Haven** is a primate rescue centre housing lar gibbons, marmosets and more, as well as owls, tortoises, meerkats and reptiles. There are keeper talks throughout the day and opportunities to get up close with the animals, and there's also a tea room, ice cream shack and picnic areas on site.

Newport Roman Villa

MAP P.38
Cypress Rd, PO30 1HA. 10min walk from town centre. http://iwight.com/Visitors/Where-to-go/Newport-Roman-Villa. Charge.

If you take the signposted walk (roughly 10mins) just south of Newport you'll come across the remains of a **Roman villa**. The remains are believed to be that of a farmhouse dating back to 280 AD and today it's (mostly) enclosed by a purpose-built museum. Inside you can see ancient hypocaust underground heating systems – an ingenious Roman invention – along with reconstructed sections of the villa that the farmhouse once belonged to.

Carisbrooke Castle

MAP P.36
Castle Hill, PO30 1XY. Bus #6, 7, 12 or 38 pass nearby. www.english-heritage.org.uk/visit/places/carisbrooke-castle. Charge.
Carisbrooke Castle is one of the Isle of Wight's most prominent attractions, mostly famous for being the 'prison' where King Charles I was kept in 1647 prior to his execution in London in 1649. Pay a visit to this English Heritage site today and you'll find a museum, Edwardian-style gardens and tranquil chapel. Greet the donkeys at the sixteenth-century well-house,

Carisbrooke Castle

before strolling along the Norman wall to marvel at the views – for once, not of the sea – across inland Isle of Wight.

The Shipwreck and Maritime Museum

MAP P.36

Arreton Barns Craft Village, Main Rd, PO30 3AA. Bus #8 from Newport or Sandown. http://shipwreckcentre.com. Charge.

The Shipwreck and Maritime Museum is made up of three galleries which look at the Isle of Wight's maritime history. Gallery 1 focuses on prehistory and Gallery 2 on shipwreck discoveries, while and Gallery 3 (the main gallery) displays exhibits on historic diving equipment, local shipwrecks and ship models. The museum lies four miles south of Newport and leads on nicely to the Arreton Down Nature Reserve.

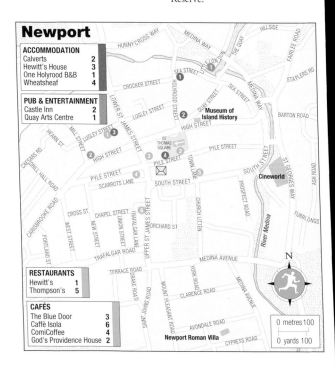

Newport

ACCOMMODATION
Calverts	2
Hewitt's House	3
One Holyrood B&B	1
Wheatsheaf	4

PUB & ENTERTAINMENT
Castle Inn	2
Quay Arts Centre	1

RESTAURANTS
Hewitt's	1
Thompson's	5

CAFÉS
The Blue Door	3
Caffè Isola	6
ComiCoffee	4
God's Providence House	2

Museum of Island History

Cineworld

Newport Roman Villa

0 metres 100
0 yards 100

An ancient woodland at the bottom of the sea

Some 8,000 years ago, the Solent was actually a valley called Bouldnor Cliff, with a river running through it. Archaeological divers (with the unlikely help of a lobster) have since discovered ancient woodland, worked flint and parts of a log boat some 40 feet down. It's thought the site was once an ancient Mesolithic hunting camp and is commonly dubbed the oldest boat-building yard in the world; find out more in Gallery 1 at the Shipwreck and Maritime Museum.

The Garlic Farm

MAP P.36

Mersley Lane, Newchurch, PO36 0NR. http://thegarlicfarm.co.uk. Charge.

Set in the beautiful Arreton Valley, Garlic Farm lies around four miles southeast of Newport. Take a Garlic Farm tour by foot or tractor and if you want to take some of the good stuff back home with you, there's plenty to choose from at the on-site farm shop: garlic ice cream, garlic mayonnaise and even black garlic vodka. The restaurant and cafe serve garlic-infused dishes (no surprises there) but there's no such thing as too much garlic as far as the farm is concerned – which is probably why their annual garlic festival is so popular (August; http://garlicfestival.co.uk). Look out for their products in shops and ingredients on menus throughout the island.

Robin Hill Country Park

MAP P.36

Downend, PO30 2NU. http://robin-hill.com. Bus #8 from Newport to Sandown. Charge.

Set in 88 acres of woodland, **Robin Hill Country Park** is pure family fun. Why not whizz along the island's only toboggan run, scamper along the 34-foot-high Jungle Heights or catch one of the amazing daily falconry

The Garlic Farm

The Isle of Wight Festival

The original **Isle of Wight Festival**, held in 1968, was a one-day hippy gathering near the village of Godshill, with Marc Bolan and T-Rex and Jefferson Airplane playing to a crowd of around 10,000 people. The following year the festival moved to Wootton near Ryde, and hosted artists such as Bob Dylan and The Who, attracting an audience of around 150,000 people. However, the 1970 concert broke all records with an estimated 600,000 people swaying to performers such as Joni Mitchell, Miles Davis, Leonard Cohen, The Doors and Jimi Hendrix at East Afton Farm (clearly visible today from Tapnell Farm). The 1970 festival remains the largest festival ever held in the UK, but it faced problems from the outset. The following year the "Isle of Wight Act" was passed, preventing gatherings of more than five thousand people on the island without a licence. This put paid to the festival for 22 years, until it was revived in 2002 at its current venue near Newport.

displays? Whether you want to walk along the Canopy Sky Walk or a sunken walkway with waters parting around you, this expansive site accommodates everyone: all aboard the Cows Express train ride, sturdy those sea legs on a pendulum pirate ride, and scamper up the Squirrel Tower.

Isle of Wight Steam Railway

Isle of Wight Steam Railway

MAP P.36
Havenstreet, PO33 4DS. Bus #9 from Newport. http://iwsteamrailway.co.uk. Charge.

The **Isle of Wight Steam Railway** sets off from Wootton Common through rolling countryside to Smallbrook Junction, and is a fab

Robin Hill Country Park

way to feel like you've travelled back in time and take in the picturesque views. The trains are all renovated steam engines, many retired from previous service on the island, with some dating as far back as the nineteenth century.

The main station is at Havenstreet, where more fun for all ages awaits and there's also a lovely four-mile stroll from Wootton station, which circles through the woodland and back to the station (or nearby pub).

The Wight Military and Heritage Museum

MAP P.36
490 Newport Rd, PO31 8QU. Bus #1, #51 or #52 to County Showground. http://wmahm. org.uk. Charge.

At **The Wight Military and Heritage Museum** there's a range of tanks, vehicles (including a French ambulance), uniforms and interesting artefacts dating from the nineteeth century onwards, as well as a war-era replicated street scene – think red brick walls, service carts

and Union Jack bunting. If you're looking to ramp it up a notch, there's a shooting range (Thursdays and Saturdays only), or to keep it low-key, enjoy a good cup of tea at the on-site tearoom, *Churchills*. There's the opportunity to take a ride in either a 432 armoured vehicle or military lorry – visit the website for details on how to book.

Butterfly World

MAP P.36
Staplers Rd, PO31 4RW. Bus #9 to Butterfly World. http://butterflyworldiow.com. Charge.

Proudly promoting itself as the 'fifth butterfly farm in the world', **Butterfly World** makes for a great rainy-day option. Look out for the different types of butterflies settling on the plants and leaves around you, where you can also get to grips with their life cycle. Aside from the butterflies there are ornate Japanese and Italian gardens, and you can also feed the fish in the Koi ponds and join minibeast handling sessions.

God's Providence House

Restaurants

Hewitt's

MAP P.38
33 Lugley St, PO30 5ET. https://www.
hewittsrestaurant.com.

Stylish restaurant with a relaxed
atmosphere. Their contemporary
British cuisine is well-presented
with the likes of prosciutto-
wrapped chicken breast (£18.50)
and grilled seabass fillet (£19),
all served with enough veg to
share. They also have a small hotel
above. £

Thompson's

MAP P.38
11 Town Lane, PO30 1JU. http://
robertthompson.co.uk.

Michelin-starred chef Robert
Thompson serves light, fresh
dishes at *Thompson's*, an open-
kitchen that's clearly popular. The
modern British menu includes
smaller plates like mackerel pate
(£13) and larger dishes like saddle
of venison (£29), or you can settle
in and really push the boat out
with the £99 six-course tasting
menu. ££

Cafés

Bluebells Café

MAP P.36
Briddlesford Lodge Farm, Wootton, PO33
4RY. http://briddlesford.co.uk/bluebells.

This lovely café – once the
cattle's winter housing – serves
award-winning veal pies (£17.55),
halloumi hash (£10.75) and
homemade soup (£6.90), with
most produce coming from their
own family farm. While here,
stock up on supplies from the
farm shop and butchery and keep
your eyes peeled for upcoming
events, like cheese and wine
evenings. They host farm tours
every August, where you can
feed and pet the calves, sit in the
tractors, visit the haybarn and,
erm, see the slurry pit. £

The Blue Door

MAP P.38
18 St James' Square, PO30 1UX. http://
facebook.com/www.thebluedoorcafe.

Quirky little café on the corner of
the high street serving homemade
breakfasts, light lunches and
tasty hot chocolate. Somewhat
unexpectedly, their speciality is
"Bunny Chow", a South African
dish consisting of curry served in a
loaf of bread (from £9.25). £

Caffè Isola

MAP P.38
85a St James St, PO30 1LG. http://
islandroasted.co.uk.

Spacious coffee shop spanning
two floors where you can order
breakfast, lunch and drinks from
on the ground floor and browse
a selection of local products
upstairs. They roast their own
coffee, Island Roasted, which
can be found across the island.
They also have a small roastery
machine upstairs. Whether
you're passionate about coffee or
need a space to work from, this
is the best place in Newport to
head to. £

ComiCoffee

MAP P.38

59 Pyle St, PO30 1UL. http://comicoffee.uk.

This coffee house-cum-comic store is a relaxed place to hang out, read comics and browse memorabilia for sale. Choose between waffles (around £11), paninis (around £7) and more tempting selections. There's another in West Cowes, by the Red Jet terminal. £

God's Providence House

MAP P.38

85a St James St, PO30 1SL. http://godsprovidencehouse.com.

Housed in one of the oldest buildings in Newport, this teahouse epitomises Old-English charm with twee furnishings and touches. As is expected, they do a cracking traditional afternoon tea for two (£14.95 per person), breakfasts (from £4) and light lunches, as well as Sunday roasts. £

Pub

Castle Inn

MAP P.38

91 High St, PO30 1BQ. http://thecastleinniow.co.uk.

The Castle Inn is Newport's oldest pub, dating all the way back to 1550 and the last in England to be granted a cock-fighting licence in 1705. This old-brick building serves real ales and ciders and dishes sourced from local suppliers, with live music at the weekends. It's also believed to be haunted by the ghosts of a young man, woman and cat... £

Entertainment

Quay Arts Centre

MAP P.38

15 Sea St, PO30 5BD. http://quayarts.org.

This arts centre is housed in three converted warehouses which overlooks the harbour. Head here for a wide range of art exhibitions, pottery lessons, comedy nights, kid-friendly events... the list goes on. As you relax in their cafe bar, be sure to admire the local art which lines the walls, too.

Quay Arts

Ryde and around

Nestled between Cowes and Bembridge, Ryde lies on the north-east of the island. This is where the Hovercraft service runs to and from Portsmouth, just a short hop across the waves. There are wide-stretching views of the glittering mainland from sandy Appley Beach, which principally makes it a seaside resort (and a lot of fun at that). Once a popular Victorian holiday resort, with a shopping arcade to boot, there are still some faded Art Deco hotels and other rundown buildings that are slightly stuck in the recent past – but with a belt of beachfront restaurants, child-friendly pub gardens and enough sand for everyone, it's a perfect spot either for a day-trip or as a starting (or ending) point for your trip around the Isle of Wight.

Ryde pier

MAP P.46

Ryde's nineteenth-century pier is a major transport hub, with a train station at each end and ferries mooring against it. While you can drive or walk along to the pier's end, there's not much to do aside from picking out the details of Portsmouth just ahead on the mainland – but if you've just arrived from there, what's the point? There's much more fun to be had under the pier, instead. Weather permitting, you can explore the long sandflats under the pier at low tide and be amazed at the marine wildlife – it's unlike anywhere else on the island, thanks to rich anemone fields and sponge gardens.

Ryde pier

Ryde and around

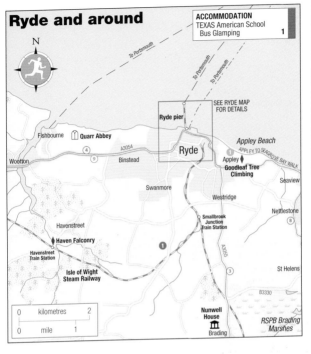

ACCOMMODATION
TEXAS American School
Bus Glamping 1

Appley Beach

MAP P.45

Lying to the east, where the sands back onto the leafy parkland of **Appley Park**, **Appley Tower** is a stone folly built in 1875, now open as a shop-museum filled with fossils and gemstones. It sits on a stretch of beach perfect for spending the day, with views looking across the Solent to Portsmouth's striking Spinnaker Tower.

Goodleaf Tree Climbing

MAP P.45

Appley Lane/Park, PO33 1ND. http:// goodleaf.co.uk. **Charge.**

Tucked away in Appley Park, just behind the beach, **Goodleaf Tree Climbing** is a great way to pass a sunny morning. The climbing takes place up a magnificent 70ft oak tree, set amid a green space of ancient woodland. Once you're dangling from the canopy, you'll have a unique panoramic of the Solent and

island coastline. It's a little tricky to find – there's no building or site centre – but is accessible by walking along the Esplanade, or through the park. There's a five percent discount for those who reach the site by foot, bike or public transport.

Haven Falconry

MAP P.45

Station Rd, PO33 4DS. https://haven-falconry.co.uk. **Charge.**

Situated at the Isle of Wight Steam Railway (Havenstreet station), **Haven Falconry** offers exciting and educational flying demonstrations. Go for walks with hawks, listen to daily talks or book onto themed experiences where you can let the feathered creatures perch on your (gloved) hand.

The Isle of Wight Bus Museum

MAP P.46

Park Road, PO33 2BE. http://iwbusmuseum. org.uk. **Free, donations welcomed.**

Hop onto a Hovercraft

Running between ports in handy locations at Southsea (Portsmouth) and Ryde, the Hovercraft is the quickest way for foot passengers to reach the Isle of Wight, with inviting, well-stocked terminals on each side. The UK's only operating hovercraft service for commercial passengers is a truly unique way of travelling to the island, and a lot of fun to boot. The Hovercraft's 'rubber ring' platform inflates before bouncing along the waves and finally landing at Ryde or Southsea. You'll find yourself raring to go with the beach, main bus terminal and a host of seafront shops at your feet.

The vintage **Isle of Wight Bus Museum** has a colourful collection of over 20 historic buses that once plied the island, including an 1880's horse-drawn stagecoach, 1940s Matador Tow Truck and 1960s Routemaster bus. While here, be sure to enjoy a refreshment at their tearoom on a former Shanklin Steamer bus. Don't miss the Rydabus Running Day either; held each May, a selection of the buses leave their garage for a special day out.

Appley to Seagrove Bay walk

MAP P.45

Make the most of the flat coastline by taking this three-mile walk from Appley to Seagrove Bay. Starting at Appley Tower, follow the Garden Walk along the sea wall (with Goodleaf Tree

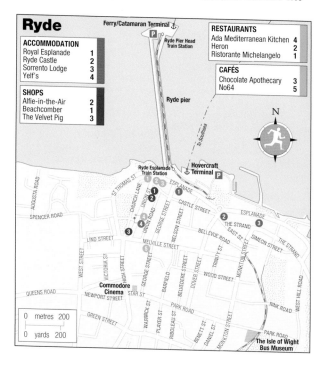

Ryde

Ferry/Catamaran Terminal

Ryde Pier Head Train Station

ACCOMMODATION
Royal Esplanade	1
Ryde Castle	2
Sorrento Lodge	3
Yelf's	4

SHOPS
Alfie-in-the-Air	2
Beachcomber	1
The Velvet Pig	3

RESTAURANTS
Ada Mediterranean Kitchen	4
Heron	2
Ristorante Michelangelo	1

CAFÉS
Chocolate Apothecary	3
No64	5

Ryde pier

To Southsea

Ryde Esplanade Train Station

Hovercraft Terminal

N

AUGUSTA ROAD
SPENCER ROAD
LIND STREET
WEST STREET
VICTORIA ST
HIGH STREET
QUEENS ROAD
NEWPORT STREET
GREEN STREET

ST THOMAS LANE
CHURCH LANE
UNION ST
UNION ROAD
GEORGE STREET
MELVILLE STREET
GEORGE STREET
STAR ST
WARWICK ST
PLAYER ST
RIBBLEAD ST
BENETT ST
DANIEL ST

ESPLANADE
CASTLE STREET
NELSON STREET
BELLEVUE ROAD
BARFIELD
BELVEDERE STREET
DOVER STREET
WOOD STREET
PARK ROAD

ESPLANADE
THE STRAND
EAST ST
SIMEON STREET
THE STRAND
TRINITY ST
MONKTON STREET
RINK ROAD
PARK ROAD
RINK ROAD

Commodore Cinema

MONKTON STREET
WEST HILL ROAD

The Isle of Wight Bus Museum

0	metres	200
0	yards	200

Quarr Abbey

Climbing on your right) and head straight until you reach Duver Road. Take the first left on Bluett Avenue, which brings you to the clinking masts of Seaview Yacht Club and take a respite at the cosy *The Old Fort* (see page 55). Then, either stick close to the coast or wind further inland to reach the final stretch on Gully Road, before culminating at Seagrove Bay.

Quarr Abbey

MAP P.45
Just outside the village of Binstead, near Ryde, PO33 4ES. Buses #4 & #3 stop outside the abbey. http://quarrabbey. org. Free.

Two miles west of Ryde, outside the village of Binstead, is one of the island's earliest Christian relics, **Quarr Abbey**. Founded in 1132, the abbey was named after the quarries nearby, where stone was mined for use in the construction of Winchester and Chichester cathedrals. You can wander freely around the beautiful grounds – there's an orchard, a woodland walk and farm animals to take in – plus you'll find a very fine teashop with outdoor tables to perch at, and a farm shop selling produce from the island. The abbey also hosts weekly-changing art exhibitions.

International scooter rally

A rather peculiar event occurs every August Bank Holiday (the last weekend in August), when up to 5000 scooters descend onto Ryde for the world-renowned **Isle of Wight International Scooter Rally**. Decked-out Vespas, Lambrettas and other scooters – think furry leopard print seats, colourful artwork, dozens of front-lights – and their riders take to the streets of Ryde and Sandown, in what is estimated as the largest single gathering of scooters in the world.

Shops

Alfie-in-the-Air

MAP P.46

8 Union St, PO33 2DU. https://alfieintheair. co.uk/.

Island-based photographer Callum O'Connell stocks an incredible array of photography prints, mostly captured using drones. Available in a range of sizes (framed or unframed), choose from landscapes of The Needles to birds-eye views of Blackgang beach waves.

Beachcomber

MAP P.46

3 Union St, PO33 2DU. www.facebook.com/ Beachcomber-1185853008206500.

Delightful coastal-themed shop selling painted driftwood, nautical trinkets and other quirky furnishings, all of which make for thoughtful gifts and unique homeware.

The Velvet Pig

MAP P.46

44 Union St, PO33 2FF. http:// thevelvetpig.com.

Vintage and retro clothing, shoes and jewellery, plus a range of quirky enamel pins. A 1980's Gucci bag or a pair of vintage Christian Dior earrings? They've got you covered. It's a real feast for the eyes: no two pieces – or customers – the same.

Restaurants

Ada Mediterranean Kitchen

MAP P.46

55 Union St, PO33 2LG. https://www. adamediterraneanryde.co.uk/.

A delicious blend of Turkish hospitality, Mediterranean cuisine and island-sourced produce. Choose from *kleftiko* (£19.95), hot and cold *meze* options from £5.50 (falafel, whitebait, *borek*) and salmon and prawn *tava* (£23.95). £

Heron

MAP P.46

2 Castle St, PO33 2EP. https://heroniow. co.uk/.

If you're looking for a unique, upmarket dining experience, make sure it's at *Heron*. Their blind-

Stone bass with Kalamata olive tapenade, roasted garlic emulsion and crispy rosti at *Heron*

Union Street

tasting menu (£85 per person) comprises seven courses selected by the chef (with wine pairing £110 per person). Otherwise, you can order individual items such as soused mackerel fillet, island-glazed pork cheek, celeriac and miso schnitzel. ££££

Ristorante Michelangelo

MAP P.46

81 Union Street, PO33 2DL. www. ristorantemichelangelo.co.uk.

A local's favourite, serving authentic Italian cuisine alongside a selection of vintage Italian wines. They also have a delicatessen shop and café. The menu is focused on the restaurateurs' background from the Emilia-Romagna region of Italy; opt for tagliatelle Bolognese (£15) or pan-fried king scallops (£23.50), washed down with a glass of *frascati superiore* (bottle £22). ££

Cafés

Chocolate Apothecary

MAP P.46

7 Esplanade, PO33 2DY. http:// chocolateapothecary.co.uk.

This yummy chocolate shop-café is set in a former Victorian fishmongers, but thankfully it's just chocolate on the agenda today. Situated just across from the Ryde Hovercraft and bus terminals, this spot sells perfectly giftable home-made chocolates or simply sip a rich hot chocolate and watch the masters at work. Bliss! £

No64

MAP P.46

64 George St, PO33 2AJ. https:// no64ryde.com/.

Whether you want a breakfast pitstop or to linger for lunch, this is one of a few new cafes cropping up across Ryde. The menu warms the cockles with vegan ramen (£8.95) and homemade soup of the day (£7.50), with other tempting options including butternut gnocchi, lentil pot pie and banana blossom nachos also worth ordering. £

The east coast

The east coast of the Isle of Wight is peppered with little villages, lesser-visited beaches and scenic walks. Pleasant St Helens is nestled between Seaview and Bembridge and provides amazing views over the bustling Bembridge harbour; the Duver, meanwhile, makes for an enjoyable stroll flanked by its sandy beach on one side and colourful beach huts and a large café on the other. As well as an abundance of nature and wildlife, you can also find out more about the historical landmarks that line this dreamy eastern coast of the island, from the Brading Roman Villa to the Grade I-listed Bembridge Windmill.

Seaview

MAP P.50

Bus #8 from Ryde

East of Ryde, the first port of call is **Seaview**; during the day it makes for a nice stroll along the seafront promenade from one town to the other, with the Solent on one side and tree-lined fields on the other. This small resort is much less brash and far more genteel, and, come summer, really gets going with the sailing and watersports scene. There are fishermen's cottages and swanky

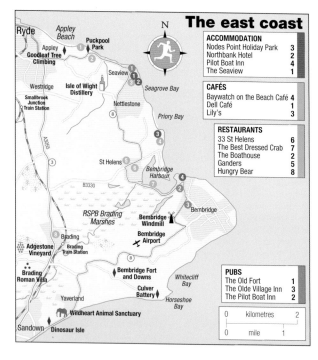

The east coast

ACCOMMODATION	
Nodes Point Holiday Park	3
Northbank Hotel	2
Pilot Boat Inn	4
The Seaview	1

CAFÉS	
Baywatch on the Beach Café	4
Dell Café	1
Lily's	3

RESTAURANTS	
33 St Helens	6
The Best Dressed Crab	7
The Boathouse	2
Ganders	5
Hungry Bear	8

PUBS	
The Old Fort	1
The Olde Village Inn	3
The Pilot Boat Inn	2

Seaview

modern houses to gaze at as you pick your way through the narrow roads, otherwise hunker down in one of the cosy pubs or continue down to Seagrove Bay and beyond.

Isle of Wight Distillery

MAP P.50

The Mermaid Bar at the Wishing Well, Pondwell Hill, PO33 1PX. Bus #8 to Wishing Well bus stop. http://isleofwightdistillery. com. Charge.

The **Isle of Wight Distillery** produces Mermaid Gin, Mermaid Pink Gin and HMS Victory Navy Strength Gin, as well as a Mermaid Vodka and HMS Victory Navy Strength Rum. The talks and tastings take place in an informal setting at a gastrobar: order a drink at the bar and enquire when the next talk is, then take your place by the glass window, behind which is the working distillery equipment. There are 10 botanicals in the Mermaid Gin, three of which are island locals (Boadicea hops, elderflower and rock samphire) and the pink and blue bottles are art pieces in themselves, made from Murano glass in Venice.

Priory Bay

MAP P.50

Backing onto National Trust-owned woods, **Priory Bay** is a 700m-long sandy strip which you can access from either Seagrove Bay or St Helens. It's extremely popular at high tide but at low tide the beach almost seemingly disappears. A delightful walk starts along Seagrove Bay's promenade, around Horestone Point and finally onto Priory Bay beach; you could continue along the coastal path, through woodland and onto St Helen's.

Bembridge

MAP P.50

Bembridge is a quiet, well-heeled village with an assortment of cafés and restaurants clustered next to the yachtie-filled Bembridge Harbour. As for the harbour itself, it's a bustling bolthole with sailing yachts, moored houseboats and eager paddleboarders. Take a leisurely stroll along Embankment Road to enjoy views of the bobbing boats with their clanking masts; the road eventually leads onto St Helen's.

Bembridge Windmill

MAP P.50

High St, Bembridge, PO35 5SQ. Bus #8 from, Sandown or Newport. http://nationaltrust.org.uk/bembridge-windmill. Charge.

Just north of Bembridge sits **Bembridge Windmill**, a Grade I-listed structure dating back to 1700. Although it looks rather dilapidated now, back in its heyday it ground the flour that was sold to the Navy and this was also where naval ships moored before they steered onwards to the Battle of Trafalgar. Naval battles aside, you can climb to the top of the windmill which lends itself to brilliant views over Culver Down, and you can also find out more about how the windmill once operated.

Brading Roman Villa

MAP P.50

Morton Old Rd, Brading, PO36 0PH. Bus #2 or #3 to Yarbridge Cross bus stop, then 10min walk (follow signs). http://bradingromanvilla.org.uk. Charge.

The award-winning museum at **Brading Roman Villa** gives modern-day visitors a glimpse into Roman British life, from well-preserved mosaic floors to extensive artifacts on display. Walk around the West Range, built around 300 AD as a winged corridor villa, and see the chalk outlines of the North and South Ranges (built between 100-200 AD) outside. Kids can dress up as Romans while everyone else takes a break at the café, whose terrace views overlook the coast.

Adgestone Vineyard

MAP P.50

Brading, PO36 0ES. https://www.adgestonevineyard.co.uk. Charge.

With a vineyard and cellars tour plus a full wine tasting lesson costing just £18, **Adgestone Vineyard** is one of the Isle of Wight's most unmissable attractions. Spanning 10 acres, this family-run business is one of the UK's oldest continuously operating vineyards, but it's not all about tradition; they also produce the UK's only blue sparkling wine. Take a guided audio tour of their subterranean cellars, enjoy cold food platters and, in the summer months,

Bembridge old windmill

The RNLI

The Royal National Lifeboat Institution (RNLI) are a registered charity responsible for providing lifeboat search and rescue services 24 hours a day, year-round. To see a lifeboat speed down the ramp on its way to a 'shout' (callout) is an incredible sight – perhaps not for the sailors in distress, but certainly awe-inspiring for anyone lucky enough to watch it from the safety of shore.

As with the rest of the UK, the RNLI depends entirely on volunteers. Below are the addresses for the lifeboat stations on the island; and don't forget to check out the small gift shops selling RNLI merchandise. With all funds going towards the RNLI, spending here is a great way to support their efforts.

Bembridge: Bembridge Lifeboat Station, Lane End Road, PO35 5TD

Cowes: Cowes Lifeboat Station, Watch House Lane, PO31 7QH

Yarmouth: The Boatshed, Quay Street, PO41 0PQ

watch daily live acoustic performances. That's not all – they also offer self-catering accommodation. Where do we sign up?

St Helens

MAP P.50

www.nationaltrust.org.uk/st-helens-duver.
St Helens is a tiny little village – one of the smallest in the country, in fact – while the Duver is just a short 10min walk from the village. With its rolling green fields, this National Trust site is a popular hiking, camping and wildlife spot complete with sandy beaches, coastal woodland walks and cragged rock pools. If you're after a scenic walk, opt for the gentle, one-mile route which sees you take in Bembridge Harbour, the Isle of Wight Golf Club and St Helens village as part of a circular trail.

Bembridge Fort and Downs

MAP P.50

Charge.

Bembridge Fort and Downs makes for another popular walking route, with a clifftop trail and its highest point at 104m (341ft). It is also home to a coastal artillery fort, used in the First and Second World Wars, to protect against enemy ships attempting to enter the Solent. For many years, it was closed to the public and used as a military zone, but nowadays it is a National Trust-owned site. While there are a couple of Second World War artefacts still visible on the headland, you will experience a much more peaceful side to the area now, with picnic benches and beautiful, wide-sweeping coastal views to appreciate – and not a warship in sight.

Horseshoe Bay

MAP P.50

Not to be confused with Horseshoe Bay in nearby Bonchurch, this **Horseshoe Bay** lies at the base of the white cliffs of Culver Down, whose familiar shape gives this small spot its name. It's advised to only try to access the beach at low tide, when the most amount of beach is exposed; it is also possible to access the Bay by boat, but only at high tide. There are also two caves nearby to check out, slightly less-appealingly named The Nostrils.

Restaurants

33 St Helens

MAP P.50

Lower Green Road, PO33 1TS. http://33-st-helens.co.uk.

Their artisan cafe serves light breakfasts, sandwiches, pastries and hot drinks, while their delicatessen offers an array of local and UK produce from fresh bread and charcuterie to condiments, dry goods and beer – perfect for an impromptu picnic on Bembridge Down. It also serves as a 'private' restaurant; contact them directly to enquire. £££

The Best Dressed Crab

MAP P.50

Fishermans Wharf, Embankment Rd, PO35 5NS. http://thebestdressedcrabintown.co.uk.

This renowned floating restaurant has been operating for almost two decades; they specialise in locally caught crab and lobster, as well as local Bembridge prawns (season only). Choose from lobster-, crab- or other seafood-filled sandwiches, salads or seriously salivating platters, with produce also available to buy from their shop. Outdoor seating overlooks the picturesque Bembridge Harbour. ££

The Boathouse

MAP P.50

Springvale Rd, PO34 5AW. http://theboathouseiow.co.uk.

With a chic beachside setting, this upmarket gastropub serves bar food, light bites, breakfast and Sunday lunches. Opt for fish pie (£16) or vegan chilli tacos (£15) and you won't be disappointed. Their garden has fantastic views across the Solent and they also offer accommodation. £

Ganders

MAP P.50

Upper Green Rd, PO33 1UQ. https://www.ganders.co.uk.

A short 10-min walk from Bembridge Harbour, this family-run restaurant overlooks the green on St Helens. Main courses – all served with potato wedges and fresh veg or side salad – include pan-fried calves liver (£21) and a vegan mushroom and aubergine bhaji stack (£17.75). Round it off with one of their homemade desserts, like a strawberry velvet sundae, or a platter of local cheeses. ££

Hungry Bear

MAP P.50

The Rectory Mansion, Brading, PO36 0DQ. https://www.hungrybear.online.

Two tips when visiting the *Hungry Bear*: book a table and turn up hungry. Their daily-changing menu offers generous servings of stacked burgers, sharing roast trays (served Wednesdays and Sundays) and more delicious concoctions. This modern restaurant is set in the Rectory Mansion, one of the island's oldest buildings. £

Cafés

Baywatch on the Beach Café

MAP P.50

The Duver, St Helens, PO33 1YB. http://facebook.com/pages/Baywatch-on-the-Beach/1456944517873609.

Average salads, veggie bites and light meals served at this café which overlooks the Solent. It's a convenient place to take a break from the beach, especially if kids are in tow, and there's also a picturesque row of colourful beach huts just a little further down the path. £

Dell Café

MAP P.50

Puckpool Sands, Seaview, PO34 5AR. http://dellcafe.com.

Set on the sea wall, **Dell Café** has a country farmhouse-style interior with views spanning Puckpool Sands and yachts gliding past on the Solent. They serve an eclectic mix of brunch, lunch and dinner options (breakfast vegan tostadas £6, surf & turf burger £13), and are very encouraging of their dog-friendly policy. £

Lily's

MAP P.50

15 High St, Seaview, PO34 5ES. www.facebook.com/LilysCoffeeShop.

There's a cosy feel to this family-run café, using grandma's recipes, milk from Briddlesford Farm and Island Roasted coffee. Choose from paninis, wraps and quiches – or one of their many sweet treats – and chill out on one of the sofas. £

Pubs

The Old Fort

MAP P.50

The Esplanade, Seaview, PO34 5HB. https://www.theoldfortseaview.co.uk.

Multi-award winning seaside pub and restaurant set right on the water's edge on the Esplanade. With a revamped upstairs and downstairs bar and restaurant inside, there's a self-service hatch and seating outside

too. Fresh, seasonal dishes include a smoked haddock risotto (£15), lamb rump (£20.25) and halloumi salad with harissa chickpeas (£12). £

The Olde Village Inn

MAP P.50

61 High St, Bembridge PO35 5SF. http://yeoldevillageinn.co.uk.

Serving real ales from across England, *The Old Village Inn* has supposedly served pints of the good stuff since 1787. There's DJ nights on Fridays, and Saturdays give way to live music nights – a classic slice of island culture. £

The Pilot Boat Inn

MAP P.50

Station Rd, Bembridge PO35 5NN. http://thepilotboatinn.com.

From the outside, the bottom half of *The Pilot Boat Inn* is styled like a ship, complete with portholes. Inside is a cosy, sleek affair, with a log-burning stove and walls lined with local artwork for sale. They predominantly serve burgers, from rosemary lamb to spicy bean, but seafood is another popular option with Bembridge crab, homemade scampi and traditional fish and chips to feast on. £

The Boathouse

The south coast

Away from Bembridge and curving towards Ventnor lie two of the Isle of Wight's most popular destinations, Sandown and Shanklin. Filled with family-friendly beaches, natural attractions, chocolate-box villages and old-fashioned charm, you could quite happily base your entire trip in this southeastern part of the island. You can get away from the hordes of crowds, too, as it goes without saying that there are also splendid coastal walking routes, especially heading east towards the headland of Whitecliff Point. There's plenty of hotels, holiday parks and campgrounds to hunker down at too.

Sandown

MAP P.58

Sandown is a traditional seaside resort town best-suited for families looking to stay put in one place, although it's not too far from Shanklin and is well-connected by public bus. Sandown has long been a beachside favourite; its five-mile stretch of beach was awarded Blue Flag status – the only one on the island – in 2022. It's a perfect spot to hone your sandcastle-building skills.

Sandown Pier

MAP P.58

The Esplanade, PO36 8JT. http://sandownpier.co.uk. Free (pier); charge (attractions).

The **pier** used to be a popular entertainment hall but is now an amusement arcade with crazy golf, bowling and a mega play area, and there's also a bar, café and ice cream kiosk. It makes for a good rainy-day option, even if arcade games aren't generally your scene.

Sandown Pier

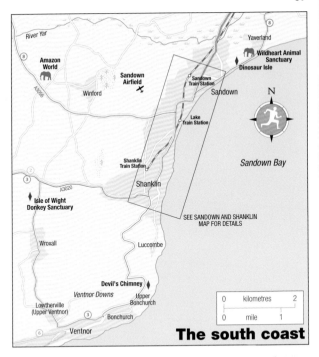

The south coast

For pretty views, walk to the end of the pier, where fishermen try their luck at catching the various species of fish and spider crabs that live beneath the pier.

Wildheart Animal Sanctuary

MAP P.57

Yaverland Road, PO36 8QB. Buses #2, 3, 4 and 24 to Newport/Shanklin. https://wildheartanimalsanctuary.org. **Charge.**
The former Isle of Wight Zoo has rebranded as the **Wildheart Animal Sanctuary**, with a focus on providing forever homes for rescued and threatened wildlife. Today it's operated by The Wildlife Trust, who also provide support for animals in India, Madagascar and the UK. They run daily walkabouts, monkey and Big Cat feeds and some reptile encounters, or you can simply walk around at your own pace. Big Cats (lions and tigers) make up the bulk of the sanctuary, but it's also home to Eurasian Lynxes, meerkats, wallabies and more.

Dinosaur Capital of Britain

The Isle of Wight is one of Europe's best destinations for **dinosaur fossils**. In 2022 it proved its status as Dinosaur Capital of Britain yet again, when 125-million-year-old bones were discovered on the southwest coast. Scientists said the bones belonged to a Spinosaurus dinosaur, a two-legged, crocodile-faced, predatory dinosaur, and marks the largest ever predatory dinosaur discovery in Europe.

Sandown and Shanklin

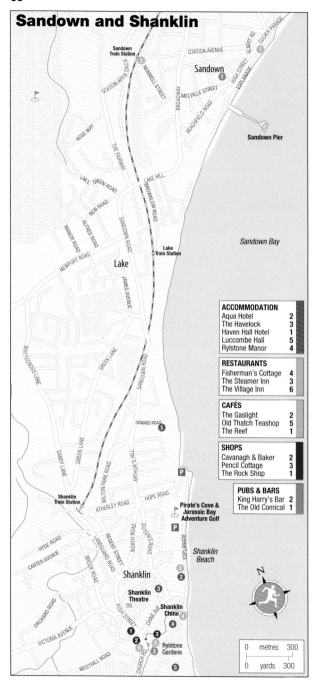

ACCOMMODATION

Aqua Hotel	2
The Havelock	3
Haven Hall Hotel	1
Luccombe Hall	5
Rylstone Manor	4

RESTAURANTS

Fisherman's Cottage	4
The Steamer Inn	3
The Village Inn	6

CAFÉS

The Gaslight	2
Old Thatch Teashop	5
The Reef	1

SHOPS

Cavanagh & Baker	2
Pencil Cottage	3
The Rock Shop	1

PUBS & BARS

King Harry's Bar	2
The Old Comical	1

Dinosaur Isle

Dinosaur Isle

MAP P.57

Culver Parade, PO36 8QA. http://
dinosaurisle.com. Charge.

Just down the road from the
Wildheart Animal Sanctuary lies
Dinosaur Isle with fascinating
displays and replicas of the various
species that once roamed (and have
been found) on the island – after
all, the Isle of Wight is one of the
best areas in Europe for dinosaur
remains and fossils, so a visit here
won't be in vain. They also host
fossil talks and handling sessions,
and it's well worth booking onto a
guided walk to discover fossils on
the beach nearby.

Shanklin

MAP P.58

Shanklin merges with Sandown,
but the two resorts couldn't
be more different – aside from
the fact they're both extremely
family friendly. It's best to tackle
Shanklin in three parts: the new
town with its high-street shops
and theatre; the memorable Old
Village at the other end with its
thatched cottages and traditional
stores; and, down the lift, steps

or chine, the beach resort, with
huge beachfront pub-restaurants
and holes of souvenir shops
selling buckets, spades and ice
creams. As well as varied nature
and geology in its cliffs, beach
and chine, you can also enjoy
interesting historic walks of
the area, or spend the evening
at **Shanklin Theatre** (www.
shanklintheatre.com).

Pirate's Cove & Jurassic Bay Adventure Golf

MAP P.58

Esplanade, PO37 6BG. https://www.
shanklinseafront.co.uk/pirates-cove-
crazy-golf. Charge.

Directly behind Shanklin's beach
you'll find **Pirate's Cove Crazy
Golf**, a perfect entertainment
option for kids and big kids alike.
The 18-hole adventure golf course
is good fun, and features pirates, a
cave, palm trees and a pirate ship.
They also have the Jurassic Bay golf
course too.

Shanklin Chine

MAP P.58

Chine Hill, PO37 6BW. http://shanklinchine.
co.uk. Charge.

Shanklin beach

The pathed stepway twisting down the tree-lined gorge known as **Shanklin Chine** is a natural wonder of beauty. The highly distinctive word 'Chine' is only used in the Isle of Wight and the neighbouring mainland town of Dorset, and is an old Saxon word meaning a deep, narrow ravine. With a waterfall at the top and a nature trail to follow down to the bottom, this steep route drops 32m in just over a quarter of a mile, and eventually leads onto the beach. You'll pass by over 150 varieties of wild plants, ferns and mosses along its nature trail, as well as a variety of birds and the elusive red squirrel. Aside from its ancient and Victorian heritage, Shanklin Chine played its part during World War II, where soldiers took part in training on the steep slopes. Down at sea level, there's a tearoom and nineteenth-century Fisherman's Cottage.

Amazon World

MAP P.57

Four miles northwest of Shanklin at Watery Lane, PO38 0LX. Bus #8 from Sandown. http://amazonworld.co.uk. Charge.

There's some 200 mammals, birds and reptiles to see at **Amazon World**, plus there are interesting daily animal talks that are worth sticking around for. Spread across the park you'll find enclosures for the likes of black howler monkeys, red pandas, greater flamingos and royal pythons among many, many others. Also on-site is a soft play area, cafe, museum and age-appropriate play areas, making this an even more brilliant option with children, capable of entertaining them for a long stretch.

Rylstone Gardens

MAP P.58

11 Popham Rd, PO37 6RG. www.facebook. com/rylstonegardens. Free.
The award-winning **Rylstone Gardens** is a lovely place to relax, with a humble bandstand, old-fashioned tearoom, crazy golf and craft cabins selling local artwork and accessories. It's a tranquil spot where you can take a breather and there's also an abundance of wildlife to keep your eyes out for, from red squirrels and cute robins to chirping birds and rare butterflies.

Shops

Cavanagh & Baker

MAP P.58

103 High St, PO37 6NS. www.cavanagh-baker.co.uk.

Emporium selling Isle of Wight-made products, from soaps and calendars to seagrass candlesticks and tea towels. Extensive wine and beer collections from the likes of Adgestone Vineyard and Goddards Brewery, and a tasty selection of jars of island chutney, pesto, pickles and passata.

Pencil Cottage

MAP P.58

22 Church Rd, PO37 6NU. https://www.pencilcottage.co.uk/.

A seventeenth-century thatched cottage where English romantic poets Keats and Longfellow once purchased their pencils (hence the shop's name). An array of gifts and souvenirs in two small rooms, which leads through to a quaint and very popular tearoom which also serves light lunches, pizzas, burgers, homemade cakes and jacket potatoes.

The Rock Shop

MAP P.58

91–93 High St, PO37 6NF. https://www.therockshopiow.co.uk/.

Be warned: this sweet shop will give your eyes toothache. The floors, walls and products are all neon-coloured and is somewhere Willy Wonka would be proud of. It takes the form of a traditional sweet shop, with huge jars filled with rock sweets, handmade fudges, and other classic sweeties, but there's also some sugar-free options. Aside from sweets, they sell a range of island specialities, including mustard, shortbread and honey. There's also a branch on the high street in Sandown.

Restaurants

Fisherman's Cottage

MAP P.58

Shanklin Esplanade PO37 6BN. https://shanklinchine.co.uk/fishermans-cottage.

Fisherman's Cottage

Nestled beneath Shanklin Chine at the furthest end of the esplanade, this thatched dining pub serves lunch, light bites and evening meals. The cottage was built by William Colenutt in 1817, who also created the pathway through the Chine just behind it, and was once visited by a young Queen Victoria. £

The Steamer Inn

MAP P.58

18 Esplanade, PO37 6BS. http:// thesteamer.co.uk.

With panoramic sea views from the veranda and a homely styled interior apt for a fisherman's front room, The Steamer Inn offers a varied menu to suit most palates and requirements: choose from jacket potatoes (£6.75) and pub favourites to vegan falafel salad (£13.95) or a gluten-free seafood chowder (£12.50). They also offer accommodation. £

The Village Inn

MAP P.58

1 Church Road, PO37 6NU. http://facebook. com/pages/Village-Inn/148572178515106. Old English charm with a darkly lit ambience, plush armchairs, grandfather clocks and a roaring fireplace. There's a bar at the centre and table service available on both floors; homemade dishes aplenty but their Sunday roasts are a real treat. £

Cafés

The Gaslight

MAP P.58

Sandown Station PO36 9BW. www. facebook.com/gaslightcafeiow.

This dinky diner-meets-tearoom hosts a range of quirky lunchtime and evening events, including vintage-themed and Northern Soul nights, and live jazz. £

Old Thatch Teashop

Fish and chips at *The Crab*

Old Thatch Teashop

MAP P.58

4 Church Rd, PO37 6NU. www.
oldthatchteashop.co.uk.

With an icing-pink exterior
and very twee interior, this is
somewhere Dolores Umbridge
from *Harry Potter* would
appreciate. The building dates
back to 1690 but today you can
enjoy various afternoon cream
teas (Victorian Tea £12.25,
£24.50 for two), home-cooked
jacket potatoes and light bites
such as a roasted vegetables
quiche (£8.50). £

The Reef

MAP P.58

Esplanade, PO136 8AE. http://
thereefsandown.co.uk.

This small, contemporary-styled
café-bar is just a stone's throw
from Sandown beach, serving up
specialty sandwiches (from £10.50),
pasta (from £12.95), salads, pizzas
and hearty mains. Whatever you
choose, cosy up indoors or take in
the great views of the award-winning
Sandown Bay on the decking.
There's a surf school next door, too. £

Pubs

King Harry's Bar

MAP P.58

6 Church Rd, PO37 6NU. www.
kingharrysbar.co.uk.

Yet another charming thatched
building in Shanklin Old Village,
with a small selection of real ales
on tap and lagers, and a garden
that backs onto the Chine walk.
There's usually hot food but it's
not guaranteed – so it's better-
suited for a swift drink than
anything else. £

The Old Comical

MAP P.58

15 St John's Rd, Sandown, PO36 8ES. 01983
403848.

Supposedly the oldest pub in
Sandown, *The Old Comical*
was established in 1859. With
a crackling log fireplace, this
inviting pub serves real ales and
there's a family-friendly beer
garden complete with a bouncy
castle. There's also regular live
music here, typically from
Thursday to Sunday. £

Ventnor to Blackgang

Although each region of the Isle of Wight has its own distinct character, Ventnor feels somewhat removed from the rest of the island – perhaps a little like a Mediterranean-on-sea, with its similar microclimate. It has long been a popular seaside resort, with the neighbouring suburbs of Bonchurch and St Lawrence making pleasant stop-offs. Towering above all three is St Boniface Down, the highest point on the island at 236m (787ft). The Down's minor landslides created the sheltered Undercliff, which gives Ventnor its very own microclimate. With excellent coastal paths, it's a perfect spot for walkers; families will have plenty of fun at Blackgang Chine funfair; and everyone else will rejoice at the charming thatched village of Godshill, one of the best on the island. With its bunting-clad high street filled with independent shops, Ventnor is also arguably the creative heart of the island, and is the home of the annual Ventnor Fringe Festival.

Ventnor Beach

MAP P.66

A walk along the Esplanade takes you past the fishing harbour, a small strip of restaurants and shops such as the island-favourite *The Smoking Lobster*. The **beach** is a rich red with never-ending

Botanical Gardens

Ventnor Beach

views across the English Channel: in fact, you are closer to Cherbourg in France than you are to London.

Ventnor Heritage Centre

MAP P.66

11 Spring Hill, PO38 1PE. www. ventnorheritage.org.uk. Charge.

On the corner of Spring Hill is the small and replete **Heritage Centre**, with interesting displays, exhibits and video footage charting the small town's history, and even a model train. You can also read about notable figures who are connected with Ventnor: Charles Dickens wrote six chapters of *David Copperfield*

in nearby Bonchurch, while former prime minister Winston Churchill spent time here as a young boy.

Botanical Gardens

MAP P.66

Undercliff Drive, PO38 1UL. http://botanic. co.uk. Charge.

Spend the best part of a morning winding your way around the **Botanical Gardens**, whose sprawling landscape features a range of subtropical vegetation. You can thank the south-facing Undercliff for this, as it gives Ventnor its own microclimate that is similar to the Mediterranean. As such, a great variety of subtropical

Ventnor Fringe Festival

Ventnor is the edgy side of the island – and we're not talking about steep cliff faces (St Boniface Down is the highest point on the island at 790ft above sea level). **Ventnor Fringe Festival** takes place at the end of July with a range of stand-up comedy, circus acts and intimate concerts performed in unique and pop-up venues, including an 11th-century chapel. Organised by Ventnor Exchange, there's also street food, craft drinks and more to add to the experience. For more information, head to http://vfringe.co.uk.

Devil's Chimney

plants grow naturally here that wouldn't on mainland Britain. You'll also find a lovely restaurant and café on site to break the day up with.

Steephill Cove

MAP P.66

A mile east of Ventnor along the coast path, or down Love Lane (past the cricket club). There's no car access to the cove, but there's a small car park on Steephill Rd, from where it is a 5min walk down a footpath to the bay.

The former fishing hamlet of **Steephill Cove** is a lovely spot to recharge, with rock pools, a beach café and seafood restaurants to explore. Away from the noise and calamity at larger resorts, Steephill Cove gives you the chance to simply sit back and watch the fishermen at work as they have done here since the fifteenth century. The place pretty much packs up over the winter

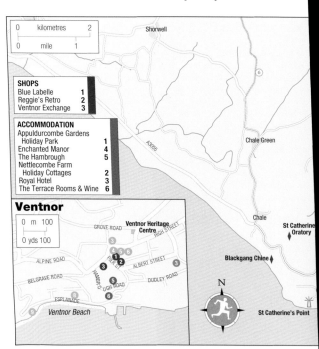

SHOPS	
Blue Labelle	1
Reggie's Retro	2
Ventnor Exchange	3

ACCOMMODATION	
Appuldurcombe Gardens Holiday Park	1
Enchanted Manor	4
The Hambrough	5
Nettlecombe Farm Holiday Cottages	2
Royal Hotel	3
The Terrace Rooms & Wine	6

Ventnor

period, though, so if you plan to visit then, come prepared with a picnic. Whatever the weather, it's a pleasant spot to wander around and take in the whitewashed cottages that roll down the rocky cliffs to the beach – which really tells you how the hamlet got its name.

Bonchurch

MAP P.66

Just over a mile east from Ventnor is **Bonchurch**, a dinky village of thatched cottages, low-set stone edifices and Victorian houses. Despite its sleepy and secluded appearance, Bonchurch has welcomed a number of prominent figures, including Karl Marx, Charles Dickens (who wrote a great deal of *David Copperfield* here).

While you're here, **Old Boniface Church** makes for a charming stop-off. This medieval church is one of the few left in England of its kind, dedicated to the Saxon

monk who died in 755 AD. Despite 'recent' renovations from the early twentieth century, you can still take in the Norman nave and chancel, while other aspects of the church are late Medieval, Tudor, Flemish and Romanesque. Once you've had your history fill, head down to Horseshoe Bay on the seafront, from where you can walk along to the Ventnor Esplanade.

Devil's Chimney

MAP P.66

PO38 1QD. 1min walk from Smugglers' Haven Tea Garden. Bus #3 to Landslip Car Park bus stop.

Less scarily known as Bonchurch Landslip, **Devil's Chimney** is a narrow, steep staircase cutting through the Undercliff, with *Smugglers' Haven Tea Gardens* at the top and the coastal path at the bottom – you can access from either way. There are handrails

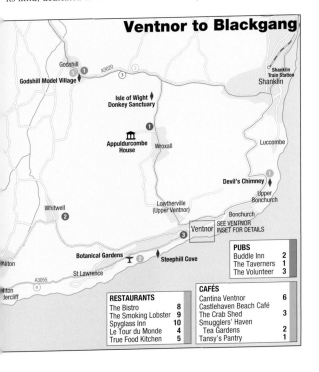

Ventnor to Blackgang

PUBS

Buddle Inn	2
The Taverners	1
The Volunteer	3

CAFÉS

Cantina Ventnor	6
Castlehaven Beach Café	
The Crab Shed	3
Smugglers' Haven	
Tea Gardens	2
Tansy's Pantry	1

RESTAURANTS

The Bistro	8
The Smoking Lobster	9
Spyglass Inn	10
Le Tour du Monde	4
True Food Kitchen	5

Godshill Model Village

at the steepest points, and it's advisable to tackle the deep cleft while there's plenty of daylight.

Isle of Wight Donkey Sanctuary

MAP P.66

Lower Winstone Farm, St Johns Rd, Wroxall, PO38 3AA. www.iowdonkeysanctuary.org. Free; donations appreciated.

The main (if not only) thing worth venturing to Wroxall for is the village's small **Donkey Sanctuary**, home to over 100 donkeys and Shetland ponies that have been rescued from unwanted homes. Seeing the donkeys in their open enclosures is a lovely way to start the day, and with 55 acres to explore, they are very well looked after. Plus, you can stop for coffee in their café, housed in a rustic barn. Not just a visitor attraction, the sanctuary also offers donkey therapy, work with children and more.

Appuldurcombe House

MAP P.66

Appuldurcombe Rd, Wroxall, PO38 3EW. http://appuldurcombe.co.uk. Free.

Just half a mile from the village of Wroxall and surrounded by tumbling fields of countryside is **Appuldurcombe House**, an eighteenth-century house that once sat in the Worsley family. With its Palladian-style exterior, renovated Great Hall and landscaped gardens (designed by Lancelot 'Capability' Brown), it's one of the most magnificent English Heritage sites on the island. An accidental landmine hit the site during World War II, but forget that – the largest thing to hit the house was the notorious Worsley Scandal: in 1782, Mrs Worsley admitted to having had 28 lovers – she even wrote a bestselling poem about it to tell her side of the story.

Godshill

MAP P.66

Buses #2 and #3.

Godshill appears as a model village itself, with quaint teahouses, thatched cottages and a medieval church setting itself as what many regard as the prettiest village on the island. On the high street, **The Old Smithy** provides a range of shops and cafés in numerous historic buildings. To make the most of the outdoors, check out the ornate garden behind the

Old Smithy, and there's also a Model Village (see below).

Godshill Model Village

MAP P.66

High St, PO38 3HH. www.
modelvillagegodshill.co.uk. Charge.
Everyone will appreciate the intricate details at the **Model Village**, with its displays of 1920s Shanklin and Godshill in micro-form and detailed landscape gardens featuring over 3000 shrubs and plants. If you're seeking somewhere quiet to enjoy a relaxed stroll, head here. When the weather's good, they open their small refreshment bar, *The Nammet Hut*, and an affordable gift shop.

St Catherine's Point

MAP P.66

Free.
Just outside Niton, **St Catherine's Point** is situated at the southernmost tip of the island. It's famed for the white octagonal lighthouse which was built here in 1838 and stands at 27m tall. Although visitors can't currently go inside the lighthouse, it's a great backdrop for the 3.5-mile walk which starts from the Old Blackgang Road in Niton to this distinctive tower – see the National Trust website for the full route.

St Catherine's Oratory

MAP P.66

Turn left at the end of St Catherine's Rd.
Free.
St Catherine's Oratory was built in 1328 and was possibly once used as a lighthouse, not far from where St Catherine's Lighthouse (see left) stands. Now owned by English Heritage, the medieval structure forms part of the Tennyson Heritage Coast and makes for another wonderfully windswept walk where you might spot grazing cows, too.

Blackgang Chine

MAP P.66

Blackgang, PO38 2HN. http://
blackgangchine.com. Charge.
The legendary **Blackgang Chine** theme park lies just two miles west on Niton's clifftop. There are rides and attractions that will suit every age here, from the Evolution pendulum swing (new in 2023) to the jiggling Pirate Barrels. The different themes of the park include Cowboy Town, Underwater Kingdom, Fairyland and Restricted Area 5, where kids can let their imaginations (and themselves) run wild. There are also regular performances from 'Blackgang's Characters' which will keep everyone entertained in one place.

The best places to stay

Although the southernmost part of the Isle of Wight is wild, rugged and remote (with natural and historic beauty aplenty), there are also a few unique places to stay in this immediate area. From Niton, drive along the winding St Catherine's Road – you can take the left turning onto Castlehaven Road for the village green, beach and accommodation – until you reach the end and turn left for St Catherine's Lighthouse (see above) or straight on to a rural farm.

Directly outside the lighthouse you will find three holiday cottages – Gurnard, Landward and Penda – which each have their own enclosed courtyard and parking space, and there's a communal grass area. Alternatively, continue straight on St Catherine's Road to reach Knowles Farm Cottage, a two-bedroom hideaway sleeping up to four guests. Whichever you choose, both are excellent bases for long walks through grassy fields with far-reaching views of the brilliant blue sea ahead.

Shops

Blue Labelle

MAP P.66

7 Pier St, PO38 1ST. http://bluelabelle.
co.uk.

Blue Labelle is a small boutique in
Ventnor, who make and sell their
own skincare products. Skincare
creams and oils are all organic
and vegan. There's also a small
selection of stocked local products,
too: think candles, local art and
upcycled bags.

Reggie's Retro

MAP P.66

5 Pier St, PO38 1ST. www.facebook.com/
reggiesretro.

Reggie's Retro specialises in vintage
and modern vinyl records. The
shop owners are more than happy
to chat or let you browse at your
own leisure – and proves Ventnor
as an innovative, independent and
talented community.

Ventnor Exchange

MAP P.66

11 Church St, PO38 1SW. http://
ventnorexchange.co.uk.

Pier Street

Part-theatre, craft beer bar and
record shop, the *Ventnor Exchange*
is a creative space promoting the
best of the community. They hold
the Ventnor Fringe Festival each
year (see page 65) and also
have a small co-working space.
You can choose to chill out with
a drink and flick through the
vinyl on sale – you might even
stumble across a *Rough Guide to
Psychedelia*.

Restaurants

The Bistro

MAP P.66

30 Pier St, PO 1SX. www.
thebistroventnor.co.uk.

Small, intimate restaurant with
an open kitchen, where food is
served in a relaxed ambience with
contemporary artwork to match.
Serving breakfast, light lunches
and dinner – we recommend the
crayfish and local crab risotto
(£12.50) or the slow-roasted duck
leg (£24.50). As there's not heaps of
room inside, its advisable to book
in advance. £

The Smoking Lobster

MAP P.66

Esplanade, PO38 1JT. http://
smokinglobster.co.uk.

Island-famous restaurant serving
contemporary Asian dishes; you'll
definitely need to book well in
advance to be sure of securing
a table. Tuck into whole ginger
and soy baked sea bass (£27), a
seafood platter for two (£90) or
stir-fried peanut noodles with
chilli-glazed tofu (£16), plus
much more. Their slick, white
interior overlooks the beach and
out across the sea, and there's
outside dining during the warmer
months. £

Spyglass Inn

MAP P.66

Ventnor Esplanade, Ventnor, PO38 1JX.
http://thespyglass.com.

Spyglass Inn

With pirate-esque and nautical decor this no-frills pub-restaurant does the job, but is better-suited to families rather than an intimate dining setting. Still, its seafront position is tempting enough (it was once a Victorian bath house) with the no-fuss menu including baguettes, burgers, lasagne and cottage pie. £

Le Tour du Monde

MAP P.66
11 High St, Ventnor. www. letourdumondeventnor.co.uk.
Seeing as you're so close to France, it's worth dining at this French restaurant, although you'll need to be quick – they only seat 20 guests on Fri, Sat and Sun evenings. Their five-course set menu includes butternut squash velouté, cod loin and thyme butter chicken, with a vegetarian equivalent menu too. Plus there's an extensive wine menu and drinks list, so you can really unwind with an evening here. £££

True Food Kitchen

MAP P.66
14 High St, PO38 1RZ. www. thetruefoodkitchenventnor.co.uk.

Offering Korean, Japanese and Thai dishes with meat, vegetarian and vegan options, *True Food Kitchen* (formerly *Tramezzini*) offers a lunch menu (bao buns £12, gyozas £8) and dinner menu (small plates from £10, mains like pork belly with satay noodles £22). They also have a five-, six- or seven-course tasting menu (from £55). Wash it all down with a drink from their Japanese-inspired cocktail menu. £

Cafés

Cantina Ventnor

MAP P.66
20 High St, Ventnor, PO38 1RZ. http:// cantinaventnor.co.uk.
Open-plan café and restaurant ideal for a casual brunch or dinner. You might be tempted by *shakshuka* (£7.50) or a Full English Breakfast (£10) accompanied with a house Negroni – they also offer bottomless brunch – while their evening menu typically includes small plates, hearty mains and naughty desserts. £

The Crab Shed

Castlehaven Beach Café

MAP P.66

Park on St Catherine's Rd and walk (10min) down Castlehaven Lane to reach it. www. castlehaven.me.uk.

Tucked away by a caravan site and moments from a small cove, this dreamy al-fresco cafe provides drop-dead gorgeous views of the sea with yachts clipping past. It's run by the people from *True Food Kitchen* (see page 71) and you can simply enjoy a hot or cold drink or Asian-infused bites, from poke bowls (£15) to tempura catch of the day (market price). £

The Crab Shed

MAP P.66

Steephill Cove, PO38 1AF. www. steephillcove-isleofwight.co.uk/ crab_shed.html.

Choose from fresh crab or mackerel pasties, served from a pretty shack with outdoor seats on the seashore. Their seafood is caught just meters away, down at Steephill Cove – keep an eye out for the fishermen bringing their haul up. No bookings as they operate on a first-come-first-served basis. Seafood doesn't come much fresher. £

Smugglers' Haven Tea Gardens

MAP P.66

76 Leeson Rd, PO38 1QD. www.facebook. com/SmugglersHaven/.

Hidden away but delightful to find, this wholesome, tranquil spot in Bonchurch offers no-frills food like beans on toast and fresh crab sandwiches at fairly reasonable prices. They have tables outside with some pretty amazing views of the Channel, and a stop here makes for a good reward after climbing the Devil's Chimney (see page 67). Veggie and vegan options are also available. £

Tansy's Pantry

MAP P.66

Church Hollow, Godshill, PO38 3HH. http:// tansyspantry.co.uk.

This plant-based, vegan restaurant-café uses local, quality ingredients to create an exciting food and drinks menu. Choose from their classic 'vish' and chips (£13), Seoul bowl (£14) and seitan chicken wings (£14), plus an extensive drinks list and vegan-friendly wines. £

Pubs

Buddle Inn

MAP P.66

St Catherine's Rd, PO38 2NE. http://buddleinn.co.uk.

The *Buddle Inn* is riddled with traditional charm, from flagstone floors to rustic inglenook beams and crackling fires in between the two. This sixteenth-century restaurant-pub is set in the island's Area of Outstanding Natural Beauty and as such serves a range of real ales and extensive homemade dishes with a view – just head out to the garden area which looks out to the sea. £

The Taverners

MAP P.66

High St, Godshill, PO38 3HZ. http://thetavernersgodshill.co.uk.

A real country pub serving award-winning cask beer on tap and a healthy selection of wines. With seasonal, local produce on the menu, pub favourites include a Goan-inspired vegetable masala (£13) and a classic Ploughman's (£12.50). £

The Volunteer

MAP P.66

30 Victoria St, PO38 1ES. www.facebook.com/The-Volunteer-386954771421365.

No, you haven't barged into someone's living room, it's just possibly the island's smallest pub. It's a very welcoming, sociable space, as all great pubs should be, but it is pretty tiny, so not suitable for larger groups or families. There's a small games room at the back, live music on Sundays and a selection of fine real ales to boot. £

VENTNOR TO BLACKGANG

The Buddle Inn

Brighstone to Alum Bay

The southwest coast is one of the least-populated areas of the island, and as a whole is largely undeveloped; there's no doubting why it forms part of a designated Area of Outstanding Natural Beauty (AONB). This is what makes it such prime walking and cycling territory, with Compton Bay and Freshwater Bay to cool off at. There's more action at Freshwater and Totland, the western tip of the island, but head out further to the westernmost tip for some of the best-known and rugged views of the island. You can enjoy this from either up high or down low: the multicoloured sand cliffs of Alum Bay, the jagged spine-like Needles and the sweeping views from the top of the headland. To make even more of the great outdoors, you can walk along the impressive Tennyson Down, named after the poet Lord Tennyson who once roamed here. Brighstone is set in the rolling countryside, and is within walking distance from the captivating gardens at the National Trust-owned Mottistone.

Brighstone

MAP P.76

The compact village of **Brighstone** is filled with low thatched cottages, the most stand-out of which can be viewed on North Street, which also includes the adorable Brighstone Village

Mottistone Gardens & Estate

Library & Museum. This genteel village is set just a little further inland from the unspoilt beach at Brighstone Bay, so you can get the wind out your ears with its leafy lanes and slower pace of life; it's all part of the island's AONB.

Brighstone Museum

MAP P.76
North St, Brighstone, PO30 4AX. Free.
You'll find **Brighstone Museum in one of these thatched cottages**, providing a detailed insight into village life. It's a small space, but they bring traditional village life in Brighstone to life with a recreated Victorian cottage kitchen, themed displays and audio recordings of villagers reflecting on their childhoods spent growing up here.

Brighstone village

Mottistone Gardens & Estate

MAP P.76
Mottistone, PO30 4EA. http://nationaltrust.org.uk/mottistone-gardens. Charge.
Six acres of formal, terraced gardens with a burst of colourful flowers await you at **Mottistone Gardens & Estate**. Located three miles or so west of Brighstone, the peaceful gardens are part of a 650-acre estate, surrounding an Elizabethan manor house. Bringing it ever-so slightly up to date is the Art Deco cabin 'Shack', once a former architects office but now an organic kitchen garden and tea garden. Among the flora on display here are olive groves, shrub-filled banks and exotic plants.

Tapnell Farm

MAP P.76
Tapnell Farm, Newport Rd, PO41 0YJ. http://tapnellfarm.com. Charge.
At **Tapnell Farm** you can meet the animals, tackle a climbing wall and whizz down the sledge slides, alongside plenty of other activities. There are wallabies and meerkats, alpacas and farmyard animals to interact with; the farm is also home to a variety of accommodation types. Also on-site is the island's only football golf course and an Aqua Park (separate charges apply).

Farringford

MAP P.76
Bedbury Lane, Freshwater Bay, PO40 9PE. http://farringford.co.uk. Charge.

Coastal trail: Colwell Bay to Totland Bay

Start at Colwell Bay at *The Hut*, a beachfront café popular with passing celebs. The concrete trail will see you pass colourful beach huts on your left and views of Bournemouth on your right. It takes about 15mins to reach Totland Bay, before ending the route with lunch or a drink at *The Waterfront*, a pleasant restaurant overlooking the Bay.

Historic-house-turned-hotel, **Farringford** was the main residence of Lord Tennyson between 1856 to 1892, and remained in Tennyson family possession until 1945. Today, you can take guided house tours of this Grade I-listed building, as well as a visit to the well-kept gardens. Pre-booking onto a house tour is advised. They also offer self-catering cottages.

Dimbola Lodge

MAP P.76

Terrace Lane, Freshwater Bay, PO40 9QE. http://dimbola.co.uk. Charge.

While many are happy to dive into Freshwater Bay and schlep along Tennyson Down, few think to travel a little further inland from the Bay. They'll miss out on **Dimbola Lodge**, the house-turned-museum of pioneering Victorian photographer Julia Margaret Cameron. After

visiting friend Lord Tennyson here in Freshwater in 1860, she moved to this spot – right by the public footpath entrance to the Tennyson Down – and today you can marvel at the same views as she once did. Inside the house, the rooms are arranged by photographs of her various contemporaries, from Charles Darwin to Robert Browning. Aside from Julia's work there are also displays and items regarding the history of photography, her reconstructed bedroom and temporary art exhibitions. Once you've finished mooching around, head back downstairs to their quaint tearoom for a pleasant view over the Downs and sea ahead.

Tennyson Down

MAP P.76

Tennyson Down was named after the Victorian poet Alfred Tennyson, who resided in

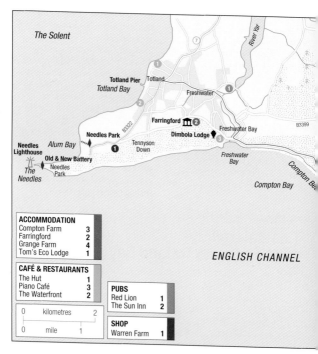

The Solent

Totland Pier · Totland
Totland Bay

Freshwater

Farringford 🏛 **2**
Dimbola Lodge 📍

B3399

Needles Lighthouse · Alum Bay · Needles Park
Old & New Battery
The Needles · Needles Park

Tennyson Down

Freshwater Bay

Freshwater Bay

Compton Bay

Compton Bay

ENGLISH CHANNEL

River Yar

ACCOMMODATION	
Compton Farm	3
Farringford	2
Grange Farm	4
Tom's Eco Lodge	1

CAFÉ & RESTAURANTS	
The Hut	1
Piano Café	3
The Waterfront	2

PUBS	
Red Lion	1
The Sun Inn	2

SHOP	
Warren Farm	1

0   kilometres   2

0   mile   1

Tennyson Down

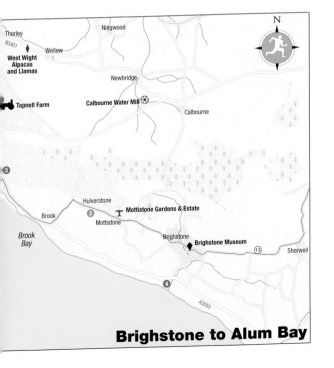

Brighstone to Alum Bay

Freshwater after relocating from London. He enjoyed walking across the downs (who wouldn't?) and today there stands a monument to him at the highest point of the clifftop, a marble Celtic cross. And what an idyllic stretch of downs to bear your name, with its strong gusts of salt air, cliff-nesting birds and copious pinpricks of wildflowers. There's a well-marked path you can follow that leads onto the Needles. Dogs are welcome on leads; it's not possible to let them run free at present, because of the various livestock and wildlife that's currently being reintroduced to the Downs.

Alum Bay

MAP P.76

Alum Bay sits at the island's western tip and is one of the most picturesque spots on the island, with a view of the Needles in the near-distance. The multi-coloured sand cliffs, for which the area is known (and where Victorian locals got their paint pigments from) consist of three minerals (quarts,

felspar and mica), due to millions of years' worth of rising seabed, eroding and sinking beneath the sea, and bedrocks causing these sediments to form the cliffs you see today. An Alum Bay sand-filled glass jar makes for a fun souvenir.

Needles Park

MAP P.76

Alum Bay, PO39 OJD. http://theneedles. co.uk. Free.

The Needles is the most iconic place to visit on the Isle of Wight. At the top of the cliff is **Needles Park**, which consists of various attractions suitable for children and there's also a viewing platform for uninterrupted views of the famous chalk stacks. More will enjoy the views to be had from the **chairlift (charge)** at the cliff down to Alum Bay. Aside from the attractions, the Needles Park is a good place to enjoy a picnic, otherwise there are a couple of shops and cafés to enjoy the views from.

Old Battery

MAP P.76

West High Down, PO39 OJH. http://

The Needles and Alum Bay

The link to the mainland

The Needles are three jagged chalk stacks that jut out of the island's western headland at 30m high. There was a fourth stack, but this collapsed during a colossal storm in 1764 – its rumblings were thought to have been heard in Portsmouth. Although you can't see it, the chalk spine continues underneath the sea floor and emerges again at Dorset's Isle of Purbeck. If you stand at the top of either site, you'll see how the two were once connected.

But thousands of years ago, the sea levels changed, and erosion caused upheaval which disconnected the island from the mainland. Before the Isle of Wight became an island, what is now the Solent (the stretch of sea between the island the mainland), was the River Solent; this huge stretch of saltwater now separated the island from the mainland.

nationaltrust.org.uk/needles-old-battery-and-new-battery. **Charge.**
Stretch your legs to the lookout at **Old Battery**, a Victorian coastal defence fort. Built in the nineteenth century to defend Britain from French invasion, the fort was also in use during both world wars. You will also find the remains of the original lighthouse here (dating back to 1786) that once warned incoming sailors about the rocky outcrops they needed to avoid. Modern-day sailors needn't worry, as it has since been replaced with a 'new' (1859, that is) one at the end of the Needles, the red and white hoops vivid against the white chalk stacks and making for a striking photo.

New Battery

MAP P.76
http://nationaltrust.org.uk/needles-old-battery-and-new-battery. **Free.**
The **New Battery** was built in 1895 as a replacement for the Old Battery – where there had been concerns about its position causing the cliffs to crumble – and was built higher up the cliff and 120m above sea level. It then went onto become a top-secret military rocket-testing site between 1955 and 1971 (during the Cold War); following this, it become a significant site for researching early space technology, and in 1971

the single all-British satellite was launched into orbit.

Totland

MAP P.76
The next bay on from Alum Bay is **Totland Bay**, which makes for a scenic walk along its seafront promenade. As you walk north towards Compton Bay, the northern views of the mainland (Bournemouth) creep into view. You'll have to head inland before coming down onto the bay by the *Waterfront* restaurant.

Compton Bay

MAP P.76
Sunbathe on the sand or lay back on the grassy clifftop at **Compton Bay**. West of Brighstone, this is one of the lesser-developed parts of the island, but that doesn't mean it's any less busy. With its crashing waves and perfect location, it's a popular spot with surfers, bodyboarders and anyone else who wants to make the most of the waves.

This is also one of the best spots to find dinosaur fossils; there are the three-toed footprints of Iguanodon at the cliff base east of Compton Bay car park at Hanover Point, between 985–1968ft wide. Tours and walks can be organized – see http://visitisleofwight.co.uk for more information.

Shop

Warren Farm

MAP P.76
Alum Bay New Rd, PO39 0JB. http://
warrenfarmiow.co.uk.

Lovely family-run farm (for
over 50 years) with a farm shop
and tea gardens. They produce
beef from their own herd of
Hereford cross cows that graze
the fields, with the Needles as a
backdrop on their 150-acre farm.
Their outdoor seating overlooks
the equally pleasant Tennyson
Down, but there's also covered
seating. Take a respite here after
a visit to the Needles and enjoy
their variety of hot and cold
drinks, cakes, snacks – then
buy some of the local produce
(including eggs, cheese or their
own beef).

Restaurants

The Hut

MAP P.76
Colwell Bay, PO40 9NP. http://
thehutcolwell.co.uk.

Diners at *The Hut*

Upmarket beachfront restaurant
popular with celebrities, serving a
seafood-heavy menu; expect items
like poke bowls, shellfish spaghetti
and grilled lobster. A converted
vintage Land Rover serves as the
'Hut Truck' which ferries patrons
to and from Yarmouth Harbour
Office. ££

The Waterfront

MAP P.76
Totland Bay, PO39 0BQ. www.
waterfrontiow.com.

Restaurant with amazing views over
Totland Bay – especially at sunset.
The building previously served
as a church, reading room and
library. It now serves a mixture of
Mediterranean and British foods,
and has a bar with live music on Fri
and Sat nights. £

Café

Piano Café

MAP P.76
Gate Lane, Freshwater, PO40 9PY. http://
thepianocafe.co.uk.

Named after Queen Victoria's
piano tuner, who once owned

The Red Lion

the building, it's now a stylishly decorated café, bar and meze restaurant. They serve breakfast, lunch and dinner and you'll also be treated to monthly live music nights, plus a variety of other exciting events. £

Pubs

Red Lion

MAP P.76
Church Place, Freshwater, PO40 9BP. www.redlion-freshwater.co.uk.
This attractive traditional pub has log fires, real ales and a lovely big garden. Choose from an award-winning menu; lunch options include a plant-based burger (£14) and mixed meats deli boards (£16), while dinner options include handmade steak and ale pie (£15.50) and whole plaice (£17). £

The Sun Inn

MAP P.76
Hulverstone, PO30 4EH. http://sunhulverstone.co.uk.
A cosy, dog-friendly pub with a thatched roof and a garden. This sixteenth-century pub serves lunch (sandwiches and ciabattas from £7) and mains like mussels and village bakery bread (£16) or aubergine and chickpea tagine (£14). £

Yarmouth and around

The northwestern town of Yarmouth sits at the mouth of the River Yar and makes for an attractive arrival point to the island. Originally known as Eremue ("muddy estuary"), the settlement is one of the very oldest on the island, dating back to at least 991, with a Norman grid system still in place today. Yarmouth is encompassed by a river one side and marshland the other, with the sea looking north towards the mainland. It's an ideal starting point to venture to the likes of ancient Newtown and the trickling-stream village of Calbourne, which you'll find slightly further inland. Yarmouth itself has a good selection of places to eat, drink and stay, but it's tightly knitted with a village square-like feel, so won't take you too long to explore what it has to offer. However, you'll soon be drawn to the town's beguiling history and will find it easy to nestle in with the village-like community. This is somewhere you'll want to linger, or at least consider returning to for a pleasant day trip; Yarmouth is conveniently linked to Lymington in the New Forest (see page 98) by car ferry, which pulls in alongside the picturesque marina, making it an easy day trip from the mainland.

View over Yarmouth

Yarmouth Pier

Yarmouth Castle

MAP P.87

Quay St, PO41 0PB. www.english-heritage.
org.uk/visit/places/yarmouth-castle. Charge.

Yarmouth Castle, the last and most
sophisticated of Henry VIII's coastal
defence forts, was intended to protect
the island from French invasion. The
town was the main port on the island
and had been burnt down by them
twice before. However, the fort was
only completed in 1574, 33 years
after his death. Today, you can look
around the inside of this sixteenth-
century castle, with reconstructed
rooms explaining how they were
used at the time, as well as displays of
various Solent shipwrecks. There are
some spectacular estuary views to be
had from the battlements.

Yarmouth Pier

MAP P.87

PO41 0NP. Charge.

The longest wooden bridge in
England still in use, this Victorian-
era **pier** still makes for a nice stroll
along, with views across the deep
water to the mainland. As you
walk back, take in the views of the
fancy waterfront houses on your
left, clinking yacht masts from the
marina on your right and chunky
Red Funnel ferry entering and
leaving harbour. The small hut at
the end of the pier is the teeny-tiny
Roundhouse Museum which details
the pier's history as and local sealife.

Fort Victoria Country Park

MAP P.84.

West Hill Lane, PO41 0RR. Bus #7 to
Westhill Lane, then a 10min walk, or 20min
walk along coastal path. www.fortvictoria.
co.uk. Free (park), charge (buildings).

Explore the peaceful walks of the
country park and along the seashore
before visiting the reptilarium,
planetarium, imaginarium and
gift shop under the arches of **Fort
Victoria**, a former military fort
which once protected Portsmouth
and Bournemouth (and the rest
of England) from attack from the
Spanish Armada. HMS *Gloucester*
is also on display, with signs telling
the tragic tale of this once-mighty
naval ship.

West Wight Alpacas and Llamas

MAP P.84

Main Road, Wellow, PO41 0SZ. Bus
#7 to West Wight Alpacas stop. www.

Newtown Old Town Hall

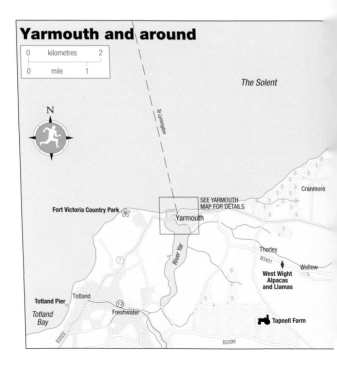

westwightalpacas.co.uk. Charge.
There are alpacas, llamas, pygmy goats, miniature donkeys, rare breed sheep, pigs, rabbits and more at the **West Wight Alpacas and Llamas farm**. You can walk an alpaca or llama and feed the lambs, before hitting the on-site café bistro for cakes, pastries and Peruvian or Island-roasted coffee.

Newtown

MAP P.84

Newtown is little more than a peaceful village – but that wasn't always the case. For 150 years it served as the island's capital, and one of the few remains of its significant past is the Jacobean **town hall** – except there's no town here anymore, just a trace of its gridded street pattern to hint at its more lively history. Dating back to the thirteenth century, Newtown is also home to a nature reserve, one of the best spots for bird-watching in

the UK. If you've explored all that Yarmouth has to offer then make the four-mile journey across to Newtown, where there are pleasant walks to be had around the nature reserve, with footpaths, a jetty and flower-covered salt marshes.

Newtown Old Town Hall

MAP P.84

Town Lane, PO30 4PA. http://nationaltrust. org.uk/newtown-old-town-hall. Charge.
The red-brick National Trust **Old Town Hall** dates all the way back to 1699, and is the only remaining evidence of the town's former importance – this was where difficult elections were held and saw two Members sent to Parliament. Nowadays, this significant building is set in an open, grassy space that forms part of the Nature Reserve. They also have the notorious Ferguson's Gang to thank for their preservation – see box for more details.

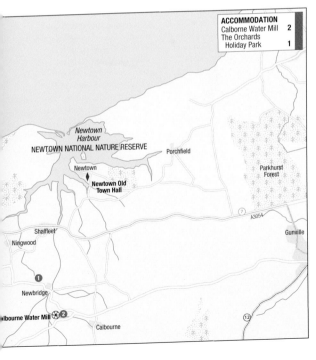

ACCOMMODATION	
Calborne Water Mill	2
The Orchards Holiday Park	1

Newtown Nature Reserve

Newtown National Nature Reserve

MAP P.84

www.nationaltrust.org.uk/visit/isle-of-wight/newtown-national-nature-reserve-and-old-town-hall. Charge.

The **Newtown National Nature Reserve** is little changed, with its field patterns reflecting its Medieval origins. It's also the only such reserve on the island, with harbourside and woodland walks, carpets of meadows and tall grass, and an abundance of wildlife. In the 1960s, there was a threat of it becoming a nuclear power station; but with local intervention it was finally left alone. Today it's a National Trust site with occasional guided walks around this quiet backwater.

Calbourne Water Mill

MAP P.84

Westover, Calbourne, PO30 4JN. http://calbournewatermill.co.uk. Charge.

Five miles southeast of Yarmouth lies the charming village of Calbourne. One of its most picturesque streets is Winkle Street, a line of thatched cottages blanketed with green ivy overlooking the trickling stream. Another mile outside of the village is **Calbourne Water Mill,** which is included in the historic Domesday Book and is the oldest working water mill on the island. Things to do and see here include milling demonstrations, adventure golf and an ancient oak woodland to explore, plus plenty more.

Meet Ferguson's Gang

You probably haven't heard of **The Ferguson's Gang**; a notorious 'gang' of five women who formed in 1927 to raise awareness and funds for the National Trust. They were passionate about protecting and preserving important buildings and land under threat – one of their acts included purchasing **Newtown Old Town Hall** and gave it to the National Trust. Although they used pseudonyms to remain anonymous, they received UK-wide press coverage for their outlandish ways of sending donations, like delivering the 'swag' inside a fake pineapple. You can read about their exploits in a small book that's on display at the Old Town Hall.

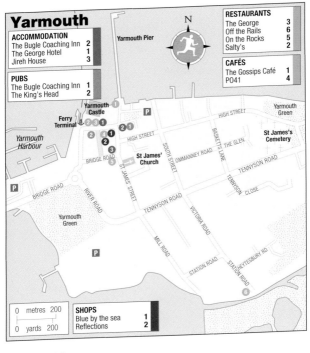

Yarmouth

ACCOMMODATION
The Bugle Coaching Inn	2
The George Hotel	1
Jireh House	3

PUBS
| The Bugle Coaching Inn | 1 |
| The King's Head | 2 |

RESTAURANTS
The George	3
Off the Rails	6
On the Rocks	5
Salty's	2

CAFÉS
| The Gossips Café | 1 |
| PO41 | 4 |

SHOPS
| Blue by the sea | 1 |
| Reflections | 2 |

Winkle Street, Calbourne

Shops

Blue by the sea

MAP P.87

Quay St, PO41 0PB. www.bluebythesea.co.uk.
Boutique store selling clothing, homemade local jewellery and niche coastal-themed items. Take a seat if they're free – otherwise the owner's two dogs are probably napping there.

Reflections

MAP P.87

1A Wheatsheaf Lane, Yarmouth, PO41 0PF.
www.reflectionsisleofwight.co.uk/.
A blink-and-you'll-miss-it shop selling fossils, crystals and minimal specimens from around the world. From wannabe fossil-finders to professional geologists, there's something for everyone – with reasonable prices to boot. Don't miss their beautiful jewellery range, either.

Restaurants

The George

MAP P.87

Quay St, Yarmouth, PO41 0PE. www.
thegeorge.co.uk.

The George

Swish, brasserie-style restaurant in their dedicated Conservatory, with uninterrupted views overlooking the Solent. Expect great food; there's pumpkin trofie pasta (£20), roasted monkfish with lobster sauce (£34) and oysters (from £18.50) to salivate over. Sit out at their beach bar during the summer and cosy up by the crackling fireplace in the lounge during winter. ££

Off the Rails

MAP P.87

Station Rd, PO41 0QX. www.
offtherailsyarmouth.co.uk.
Close to the Yarmouth Ferry Terminal, this unique restaurant is set along the line of Yarmouth's old train station. Pop in for a bacon roll (£6.95), or their on-theme named dishes, like a gluten-free Platform (Lebanese chicken £18), Controller's Chowder (£19) or Bullet Train (Tonkotsu ramen £19). Leave room for their dessert trolley. £

On the Rocks

MAP P.87

Bridge Rd, PO41 0PJ. www.
ontherocksyarmouth.com.

As the name suggests, everything on the menu here is served on a sizzling hot rock plate. Choose from the likes of steak, scallops and halloumi (generally between £18 and £22); all dishes are served with bottomless chips and salad. ££

Salty's

MAP P.87
Quay St, PO41 OPB. www.saltysrestaurant.co.uk.
Fun, lively restaurant a stone's throw from the harbourfront. The two-floor dining spaces include long bench tables with a menu serving small plates (duck liver parfait £9), mains like artichoke risotto (£18) and sumptuous seafood like St Austell's Bay mussels (£10). For some extra local flavour after your dinner, enjoy the weekly acoustic live music lounge, which takes place upstairs. £

Cafés

The Gossips Café

MAP P.87
The Square, PO41 ONS. http://thegossipscafe.com.
Conveniently located next to the pier, this coffee shop serves sandwiches, salads, stone-baked pizzas and crab specialities, as well as a range of soft, hot and alcoholic drinks. The interior is slick, airy and spacious, and outdoor seating is also available. £

PO41

MAP P.87
St James Court, Quay St, PO41 OPB. www.facebook.com/PO41CoffeeHouse.
Small, independent coffee shop that fills up quickly, serving freshly roasted coffee and light lunches. Their roastery is based in a young offender's prison, HMP Feltham Young Offenders Institute, with a mission to train the inmates in coffee roasting and barista skills. £

The King's Head

Pubs

The Bugle Coaching Inn

MAP P.87
The Square, PO41 ONS. www.characterinns.co.uk/the-bugle-coaching-inn.
A charming, cosy pub popular with locals, yachties and their dogs; they also serve hearty mains including smoky hunters' chicken (£15) and butternut squash risotto (£13). Perfect after a day in the fresh air. The pub is also known for offering good-value daily special deals, which run from Wednesday curry nights to amazing Sunday roasts. £

The King's Head

MAP P.87
Quay St, PO41 OPB. www.characterinns.co.uk/the-kings-head.
Cosy pub with a charming, low-timbered ceiling, offering a selection of hearty pub classics like a 'chilli non carne' (£13.50), liver and bacon (£14) and beef and Guinness stew (£15). Make sure to keep an eye on their Facebook page for regular live music fixtures. £

Further afield

It can be easy to forget that there's a world outside of the Isle of Wight. The mainland points that provide transport links with the island – Portsmouth, Lymington and Southampton – all lie along the south coast and are each worth exploring in their own right; or you can easily add it on as a visit to the beginning or end of your trip to the Isle of Wight. After all, a visit to the Isle of Wight embraces slow travel, which will leave you wondering what all the rush is for, so there's no better way to continue this than by taking the time to explore these south coast towns and cities. They are filled with ancient forests, historic ruins, trendy dining spots and long stretches of beach, to name a few, and serve as a great base to explore further by foot or public transport. From the fauna of the New Forest to the family-friendly festivals in Southsea, you could happily spend a couple of extra nights on the mainland as a precursor or way to round-off your visit to the Isle of Wight. Portsmouth is well worth a weekend to revel in its fascinating naval history, enjoy a slice of cake in its quirky tearooms and get to grips with the local pub scene; Southampton provides great shopping and history spots; and a trip to Lymington and the New Forest is the perfect way to reconnect with nature, wildlife and the great outdoors.

The Spinnaker Tower and Gunwharf Quays

Spitbank Fort and the Isle of Wight ferry

Brief history

One of two great maritime bases, **Portsmouth** was founded around 1180 AD and played a significant role in various historic events, from Nelson's last battle at Trafalgar to a major launchpad for the D-Day landings. The other, **Southampton**, saw King Henry V depart from this major port in 1415 for a French campaign resulting in the Battle of Agincourt. As well as still-standing medieval walls, the city is famed as being the departure point of the ill-fated *Titanic*'s maiden (and only) voyage. Last but not least, the bucolic **New Forest** was a former royal hunting ground but today these managed woodlands are a great way to get off the beaten track.

Portsmouth

Britain's foremost naval station, **Portsmouth** occupies the bulbous peninsula of Portsea Island, its harbour clogged with naval frigates, ferries bound for the continent or the Isle of Wight and avid sailors. Due to its military importance, Portsmouth was heavily bombed during World War II, and only **Old Portsmouth**, based around the original harbour,

What have the Romans ever done for Portchester?

Six miles northwest of Portsmouth city centre lies the Roman-built **Portchester Castle**. The English Heritage site is well-worth visiting, bearing the finest example of Roman walls in northern Europe. Later additions were made in the medieval age and there's also a church with a small, lovely tearoom. Today, you can climb to the top of the Castle or simply pack a picnic and enjoy the grassy expanses that the walls surround.

HMS *Victory*

preserves some Georgian and a little Tudor character. East of here is **Southsea**, a lively suburb of terraces with a shingle beach, seaside amusements, independent tearooms and pub-life in Albert Road reigning supreme.

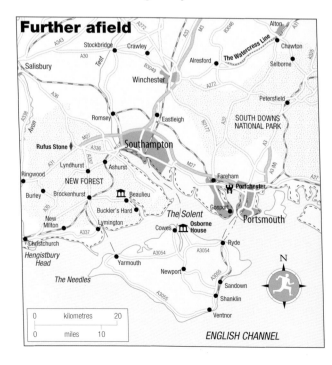

Further afield

Salisbury
Stockbridge
Crawley
Alton
Chawton
The Watercress Line
Alresford
Selborne
Winchester
Petersfield
SOUTH DOWNS NATIONAL PARK
Romsey
Eastleigh
Rufus Stone
Southampton
Lyndhurst
Ashurst
Ringwood
NEW FOREST
Fareham
Porchester
Burley
Brockenhurst
Beaulieu
Gosport
Buckler's Hard
The Solent
Portsmouth
New Milton
Lymington
Cowes
Osborne House
Christchurch
Ryde
Hengistbury Head
Yarmouth
Newport
Sandown
The Needles
Shanklin
Ventnor

| 0 | kilometres | 20 |
| 0 | miles | 10 |

ENGLISH CHANNEL

Spinnaker Tower

Gunwharf Quays, PO1 3TT. http://
spinnakertower.co.uk. **Charge.**
Moments from Portsmouth
Harbour train station (and the
Isle of Wight ferry foot-passenger
terminal) lies the shopping
complex of **Gunwharf Quays**,
where you'll also find plenty of
restaurants, a cinema and bars.
Overlooking the waterfront
stands the **Spinnaker Tower**,
an elegant, 557ft-high sail-like
structure, offering **views** of up to
twenty miles over land and sea.
There are viewing decks with a
glass 'Sky Walk', where you can
gaze down at the ant-size people
100m beneath your feet. They also
offer afternoon tea – and even the
chance to go abseiling…

The Historic Dockyard

Victory Gate, HM Naval Base, PO1 3LJ.
http://historicdockyard.co.uk. **Charge.**
For most visitors, a trip to
Portsmouth begins and ends at the
Historic Dockyard, in the **Royal
Naval Base** at the end of Queen
Street. The complex comprises
three ships and several museums,
with the main attractions being

HMS Victory, HMS Warrior, the
National Museum of the Royal
Navy, the Mary Rose Museum,
and a boat tour around the
harbour. One of the working
docks, No.9 Dock, was even used
in the filming of *Les Misérables*
(2013).

HMS Warrior

Portsmouth Historic Dockyard's
youngest ship, **HMS** *Warrior*,
dates from 1860. It was Britain's
first armoured (iron-clad)
battleship, complete with sails and
steam engines, and was the pride
of the fleet in its day. Explore the
ship's four decks and take in the
displays of weaponry, including
rifles, pistols and sabres.

HMS Victory

HMS *Victory* set sail from
Portsmouth for Trafalgar on
September 14, 1805, and
although it returned in triumph
three months later, it carried the
corpse of Admiral Nelson, who
had been shot by a sniper from
a French ship. you can see a
plaque on the deck marking the
spot where Nelson was fatally

HMS Warrior

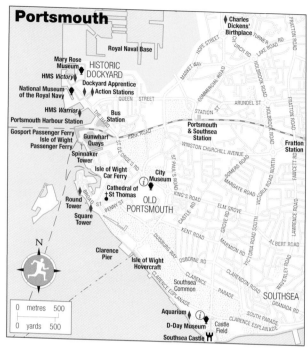

Portsmouth

The Mary Rose museum

wounded and you can also see the wooden cask in which his body was preserved in brandy for the return trip to Britain. Today HMS *Victory* stands in the dry dock beside the modern Mary Rose Museum.

National Museum of the Royal Navy

Opposite the HMS Victory, various buildings house the exhaustive **National Museum of the Royal Navy**. Over 2.5 million items trace the story of the Royal Navy from its origins in 625 AD to the present day. The collection includes some jolly figureheads, Nelson memorabilia (including the only surviving sail from HMS *Victory*) and archaeological finds.

Mary Rose Museum

The impressive, boat-shaped **Mary Rose Museum** was built around

Charles Dickens' Birthplace Museum

Henry VIII's flagship, the **Mary Rose**, and houses not only the ship itself, but also thousands of objects retrieved from or near the wreck including guns, gold and the skeleton of a dog, affectionately named 'Hatch'. The ship capsized before the king's eyes off Spithead in 1545, sinking swiftly with almost all her seven-hundred-strong crew. In 1982 a massive conservation project successfully raised the remains of the hull, which silt had preserved beneath the seabed, and you can now view the world's only remaining sixteenth-century warship level by level; it's truly an amazing experience.

Charles Dickens' Birthplace

393 Old Commercial Rd, PO1 4QL. http://charlesdickensbirthplace.co.uk. Charge.
Just over a mile northeast of Old Portsmouth, **Charles Dickens' Birthplace** looks much as it would have looked when the famous novelist was born here in 1812. Charles's father, John, moved to Portsmouth in 1809 to work for the Navy Pay Office before he was

recalled to London in 1815, so Charles only lived here for three years. Nevertheless, he is said to have returned often and set parts of Nicholas Nickleby in the city. The modest house not only contains period furniture – you can take in the parlour, dining room and bedroom – but also a wealth of information about the time when Dickens lived here, and the influences on his novels.

Old Portsmouth

It's a well-signposted fifteen-minute walk south of Gunwharf Quays to **Old Portsmouth**. Established in the eighteenth century, the area is also known as Spice Island, as this was the first place where spices from Jamaica arrived. From *Spice Island Inn*, walk along cobbled Georgian streets and take in beautiful historic architecture (and expensive properties), from the white Quebec Bathhouse to the Tudor-age Round Tower. The walk can be extended from the end of Old Portsmouth (by the Nelson statue) with the recent addition of a beachfront

The Overlord Embroidery at the D-Day Museum

promenade, which also takes in a Tudor-age artillery fort left in-situ.

Southsea

Southsea boasts a wide, grassy common that looks out onto a shingle beach, where the hovercraft departs from. The Common is home to numerous events and festivals throughout the calendar year, including the popular Victorious Festival in August. At one lively end of the seafront (connecting to the beachfront promenade into Old Portsmouth) lies Clarence Pier, an arcade and fairground park. At the other end is South Parade Pier, with rose gardens, a model village and Canoe Lake nearby. Further inland, you'll find a strip of bars along Palmerston Road, independent restaurants along Osborne Road and lively bars and pubs along Albert Road as well as the Grade II-listed King's Theatre. Southsea is renowned for its vintage tearooms, antique stores and the small performance venue, the Wedgewood Rooms. Independent, local-run businesses reign supreme in Southsea; you'll find few major chains here. During the summer, make a beeline for Southsea Bandstand, where live music/dance performances and DIY barbeques are the main event.

Southsea Castle

Castle Esplanade, PO5 3PA. http://southseacastle.co.uk. Free, donations welcomed.

Next door to the D-Day Museum lies Southsea's most historic building, **Southsea Castle**. It was built from the remains of Beaulieu Abbey and today you can go inside the keep and learn about Portsmouth's military history – make sure you climb up to the spot from where Henry VIII is said to have watched the *Mary Rose* sink in 1545. There's a pleasant restaurant-café called *The Courtyard* in, obviously, the courtyard.

D-Day Museum

Clarence Esplanade, PO5 3NT. http://ddaymuseum.co.uk. Charge.

The modern **D-Day Museum** focuses on Portsmouth's role as the principal assembly point for the Normandy beach landings in World War II, code-named "Operation Overlord". Inside, the well-designed route shares naval and local war-time stories, with plenty of objects and interactive displays to take in. There's a lot to see here, but don't miss the 295ft-long Overlord Embroidery, a sort of twentieth-century equivalent of the Bayeux Tapestry, which took five years to complete. The on-site café is a relaxed place to take a break.

Blue Reef Aquarium

Clarence Esplanade, PO5 3PB. http://bluereefaquarium.co.uk/Portsmouth. Charge.

If you're looking for a rainy-day option, head to the **Blue Reef Aquarium**. It's home to a variety of marine life, including tropical fish, sea horses, otters, rays and sharks. There's even a walk-through underwater tunnel – try to spot the fish swimming above you. Visitors can also attend various talks and feeding sessions that are held throughout the day.

Southampton

Southampton is home to numerous stirring events, from the Pilgrim Fathers' departure on the *Mayflower* in 1620 to the maiden voyages of the *Queen Mary* and the *Titanic*. While it's reinvented itself as a major cruise port as well as a shopping destination at West Quay, you can still see its medieval charm in parts and take in the impressive **Cultural Quarter**, with its open squares, excellent art gallery and the superb **Sea City Museum**. It's also home to the **Jane Austen Trail**, where there are eight plaques at locations associated with the novelist who holidayed and later lived here between 1806-1809.

City Art Gallery

Commercial Rd, SO14 7LP. https://southamptoncityartgallery.com/. Free.

Spanning contemporary art and historic exhibitions, the

Portchester Castle

excellent **City Art Gallery** is based in Southampton's cultural quarter. There are over 5,000 works spanning eight centuries to take in, from Renaissance and 19th-century French paintings, although there's more of a focus on 20th-century and contemporary British art, with Surrealist, Camden Town Group and St Ives School works on display.

The Sea City Museum

Civic Centre, Havelock Rd, SO14 7FY. http://seacitymuseum.co.uk. Charge.

One of the most popular attractions in Southampton, the **Sea City Museum** opened on April 10, 2012, the hundredth anniversary of the day that the *Titanic* sailed from Southampton's Town Quay on its maiden voyage. The museum provides a fascinating insight into the history of the ship, its crew and, of course, an account of the fateful journey. Other collections focus on the city's history, from Roman traders and Saxon settlers to its changing communities.

Tudor House and Garden

Bugle St, SO14 2AD. https://tudorhouseandgarden.com/. Charge.

Discover over 800 years of history at the timber-framed **Tudor House and Garden**. The late fifteenth-century building faces St Michael's Square, while the adjacent King John's Palace was built by the Normans some 300 years earlier. Walk around the pleasant Tudor gardens and venture inside the buildings to admire historic architecture as well as a range of somewhat quirky finds on display – from a medieval jewel casket to Victorian stuffed birds.

Lymington and around

Wedged between Southampton and Bournemouth, **Lymington** is the most pleasant point of access for ferries to the Isle of Wight. This harbourside haven rises from the quay area, with the cobbled street of the old town lined with Georgian

The West Quay shopping centre and medieval walls in Southampton

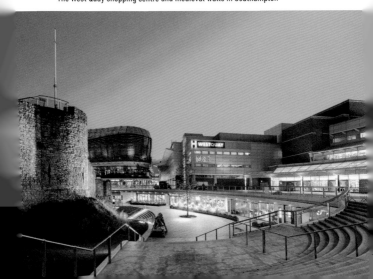

Stream in the New Forest

houses. Unmissable things to see and do here include a visit to **Hurst Castle** (the closest point to the Isle of Wight), St Barbe Museum and Art Gallery and the sea-water swimming baths. If you're hanging around waiting for a ferry, there are also some charming shops and boutiques to have a browse in, and places to grab a coffee and a snack.

The New Forest

Covering about 220 square miles, the **New Forest** is one of southern England's favourite rural playgrounds. The New Forest enjoys a unique patchwork of ancient laws and privileges alongside the regulations applying to its National Park status. The **trees** here are now much more varied than they were in pre-Norman times, with birch, holly, yew, Scots pine and other conifers interspersed with the ancient oaks and beeches. You'll likely spot a few New Forest ponies grazing nonchalantly by the roadsides and ambling through some villages. The local deer are less visible now that some of the faster roads are fenced, although several species still roam the woods, including the tiny **sika deer**, descendants of a pair that escaped from nearby Beaulieu in 1904.

Camping in the New Forest

There are 13 campsites throughout the Forest run by **Forestry England Camping** (http://campingintheforest.co.uk). Check the website for operating months, although some are open year-round. Some are very simple, with few or no facilities, others have electricity and hot shower blocks, but they all have open access to the Forest. Many have streams and fords running through them, with ponies and donkeys wandering freely.

ACCOMMODATION

Luccombe Hall Hotel

Accommodation

Self-catering cottages, slick hotels, spacious campsites, cosy B&Bs – there's plenty of places to stay on the Isle of Wight. Weather permitting, camping is one of the most immersive ways to stay on the island, with many spots in picturesque settings and sites well-catered for families. If you're looking for a little more privacy and a home-away-from-home feel, choose stays at swish or historic self-catering pads, although you'll also find reasonably-priced B&Bs and guesthouses as well. The prices we quote for accommodation in this Guide (see page 117 for price codes) generally refer to the cheapest available double room in high season (usually August), including breakfast, unless otherwise stated. Some accommodations offer discounted ferry and public transport passes, so if you're looking to save a little, it's worth considering these establishments. Note that rates rise considerably during Cowes Week (around the end of July, beginning of August) so book well in advance, but there are lower rates and usually much more choice in the off-season.

Cowes and around

ALBERT COTTAGE MAP P.28. York Ave, East Cowes, PO32 6BD. http://albertcottagehotel.com. Once part of Victoria and Albert's Osborne Estate, this Grade II-listed building is now a boutique hotel offering ten bedrooms. Set amongst picturesque acres of gardens, Albert Cottage retains a Victorian country-house ambience, with cream-coloured and wooden furniture across their double and twin rooms and suites. Also on-site is their slick *Consort Restaurant*. ££

BUSIGNY HOUSE MAP P.30. 16 Castle Rd, West Cowes, PO31 7QZ. https://busigny.co.uk/. This spacious guesthouse spans three floors and sleeps up to 18 guests: you can either rent by the room (eight in total) or the entire house itself. The attention to detail – mostly coastal-themed, of course – makes it a home away from home and is in an enviable location, just 5min from the Marina and Northwood Park. £

DUKE OF YORK MAP P.30. Mill Hill Rd, PO31 7BT. www.dukeofyorkcowes.co.uk. This no-frills B&B is just around the corner from the crossing to East Cowes and the lively high street, and is a pub in itself as well. All rooms are en suite and are pretty basic, but ideal if you just need somewhere to touch base. £

FORESTERS HALL MAP P.30 30 Sun Hill, PO31 7HY. https://forestershall.com/. Boutique hotel and restaurant with 14 rooms boasting views of the sea, the old town and their terraced garden. Individually styled rooms are seriously swanky, with a few retaining their eighteenth-century heritage features. There's a heated pool in the summer months and a new restaurant should have opened by the time you're reading this. £££

HAROLD HOUSE MAP P.30. 218 Park Rd, PO31 7NG. Sun Hill, Cowes, PO31 7HY. https://luxurycottages.com/cottages/

harold-house/. Renovated three-storey townhouse in the heart of Cowes, sleeping up to six guests with three bedrooms and two bathrooms (including a roll-top bathtub). Restored and decorated to a high standard, which is reflected in the price. £££

HOLLY TREE HOUSE MAP P.28. 218 Park Rd, PO31 7NG. www.hollytreehousecowes. co.uk. Stylish B&B with four rooms, each named after different areas of the island, with individual coastal stylings and all en-suite. You can also request the use of beach towels and umbrellas too. Great value for a great little B&B. £

INTO THE WOODS MAP P.28. Lower Westwood, Brocks Copse Rd, Wootton, PO33 4NP. http://isleofwighttreehouse.com. Two handcrafted tree houses (sleeping two to six guests) and a hideaway consisting of three exclusive huts (sleeps up to six), perfect for a spot of rugged glamping. Includes woodburners, en-suite showers and hot tubs. All self-catering, you'll feel right at the heart of nature in this peaceful setting, with plenty of space in the woods for kids to run around. Decent Red Ferry deals too. ££

THE LITTLE GLOSTER MAP P.28. 31 Marsh Rd, Gurnard Marsh, PO31 8JQ. http://thelittlegloster.com. In Gurnard, west of Cowes, sits *The Little Gloster*, a Scandinavian-styled hotel-restaurant right on the water's edge. You can choose to stay in one of three stylish guest rooms that each have their own unique selling point – duplex windows, a balcony, private sitting room – and all overlook the sea. ££

NEW HOLMWOOD HOTEL MAP P.28. 65 Queen's Rd, PO31 8BW. www. newholmwoodhotel.co.uk. This spacious hotel features 26 rooms, some with sea views, and suites include a lounge. Rooms can be adapted into twin or double rooms as necessary. Outside the front of the hotel is their restaurant, which looks out towards the Solent. Offers ferry crossing deals too. ££

UNION INN MAP P.30. Watch House Lane, West Cowes, PO31 7QH. http://

unioninncowes.co.uk. Above their popular historic pub are six small rooms (all en-suite). These are individually styled and feature one wall of printed wallpaper. What they lack in space they make up for in location: not only are you just off the high street but you're right in the heart of the action for Cowes Week, and there's a busy bar downstairs. £

VILLA ROTHSAY MAP P.28. 29 Baring Rd, West Cowes, PO31 8DF. http://villa-rothsay.co.uk. Named after King Edward VII (Queen Victoria's eldest son), who was the Duke of Rothesay when he regularly visited the Villa at the time. The likes of the drawing room and the staircase make you feel like you've been transported back to the Victorian age with its traditional decor, but the bedrooms are slightly more up to date with televisions, hot drinks facilities and modern bathrooms (including light-ringed mirrors). You can't beat the views, either – wave to the passing yachts from the balcony. They also have a drawing room, complete with wraparound balconies providing sea views. ££

Newport and around

CALVERTS MAP P.38. 27 Quay St, PO30 5BA. www.calvertshotel.co.uk. This grade II-listed building was once home to Newport's mayor, but today functions as a budget hotel with plenty of character. The rooms are pretty basic, which can be expected at the rates, but are all en suite and include a television and other basic amenities. They also have a bar, breakfast room and a large lounge. £

HEWITT'S HOUSE MAP P.38. 33 Lugley St, PO30 5ET. www.hewittshouse.com. Six spacious rooms with light-toned décor and furnishings, plus desk space. Breakfast is served either in the downstairs restaurant or tucked in the secret garden at the rear of the building. All but one of the bedrooms are en suite (one room has a private external shower room down the hall) and include flat-screen TVs. ££

ONE HOLYROOD B&B MAP P.38. 1 Holyrood St, PO30 5AU. http://oneholyrood. co.uk. Twelve spacious rooms and a

Best campsites

Nodes Point Holiday Park; see page 104
Appuldurcombe Gardens Holiday Park; see page 105
Compton Farm; see page 106
Calborne Water Mill; see page 107
The Orchards Holiday Park; see page 107

self-contained apartment (down the road) available at this B&B, which is Grade II-listed. Dining areas are shared with the public. Guests can enjoy a secluded terrace and garden that are filled with scented plants all year round. £

WHEATSHEAF MAP P.38. 16 St Thomas' Square, PO30 1SG. www. thewheatsheafhotel.com. Attractively located by a string of cafés, shops and restaurant overlooking St Thomas' Square, this hotel features bright, airy rooms – think white panelling and furniture, rolltop bathtubs, faux-fur throws – and it is also home to a popular pizzeria and Italian restaurant. £

Ryde and around

ROYAL ESPLANADE MAP P.46.
16 Esplanade, PO33 2ED. www.
royalesplanadehotel.co.uk. Undoubtedly the best location in Ryde, with some rooms overlooking the hovercraft terminal and situated in a grand, Victorian building along the Esplanade. The rooms aren't anything special but are spacious, and the hotel also has a restaurant, breakfast room and bar downstairs. They also offer decent Hovercraft and car ferry discount deals. £

RYDE CASTLE MAP P.46. The Esplanade, PO33 1JA. http://oldenglishinns.co.uk. The popular Ryde Castle sits just behind the Ryde Esplanade and as well as being a popular pub-restaurant, offers 18 rooms (all en-suite) which are spacious yet cosy, with some providing sea views. Includes accessible rooms. ££

SORRENTO LODGE MAP P.46. 11 The Strand, PO33 2LG. http://sorrentolodge. co.uk. Perfect seaside spot tucked away from the main action but still within walking distance of it all. The B&B is

housed in a Grade II-listed building and houses a few rooms including a couple of family-sized suites. £

TEXAS AMERICAN SCHOOL BUS GLAMPING MAP P.45 Hazelgrove Farms, PO33 4BD. https://www. americanschoolbusglamping.com/. Yes, you can really stay in a vintage American school bus with Retro Staycations. This quirky glamping spot sleeps up to six guests in king-sized and single beds, and is equipped with a kitchen, dining tables, book, games, firepit and eco log-burning stove. There's also a hot shower on board while outside are shared toilet facilities. Stock up on supplies at the site's farm shop. Two-night minimum stay, also offers ferry discount deals. £££

YELF'S MAP P.46. 54 Union St, PO33 2LG. www.yelfshotel.com. Yelf's was one of the island's original coaching inns, but today is a hotel, restaurant and lounge. All are en suite with basic amenities and there's free off-road parking. Rooms are decent enough, and include accessible rooms. ££

The east coast

NODES POINT HOLIDAY PARK MAP P.50.
Nodes Rd, St Helens, PO33 1YA. www.
parkdeanresorts.co.uk/location/isle-of-wight/nodes-point. Either bring your own caravans and tents or hire them here at this holiday park, which boasts an excellent position in Bembridge overlooking the bay. The facilities are excellent, with swimming pools, an arts and crafts den and bowling alley, as well as a bar-restaurant. Just remember to pull yourself away to check out the rest of Bembridge! Typically three-night minimum stay. ££

NORTHBANK HOTEL MAP P.50.
Circular Rd, PO34 5ET. http://

northbankhotel.co.uk. This boutique hotel runs down to the beach via its small sloped garden, with superlative views across the Solent. Offering 16 rooms – most of which have a seaview – the rooms are a mix of traditional and modern, with nautical details peppered throughout. As well as a daily-changing restaurant menu, there's also a lounge and bar area. ££

PILOT BOAT INN MAP P.50. Station Rd, Bembridge, PO35 5NN. http:// thepilotboatinn.com. There's no missing the Pilot Boat Inn, with its ground floor exterior styled like the blue hull of a boat – portholes and all. Inside, there are five rooms (all en suite) to choose from and all available at the same rates. With wash stations, eBike charging points and secure bicycle storage, it's a good option for cyclists and walkers. £

THE SEAVIEW MAP P.50. The High St, PO34 5EX. http://seaviewhotel.co.uk. Slap-bang in the middle of Seaview is this grandiose Victorian townhouse. The rooms vary in size and some offer sea views, but all are comfortable and the gardens run down to the beach. It's good for families and has a daily-changing menu, all homecooked and using local produce. ££

The south coast

AQUA HOTEL MAP P.58. 17 The Esplanade, PO37 6BN. http://theaqua. co.uk. Like a square chunk of chalk jutting out from the cliffside, this family-run hotel along the Shanklin Esplanade has its own brasserie restaurant (breakfast and dinner) and a sea-facing terrace out at the front. Some of the bright, modern-furnished rooms (all en suite) have their own balconies overlooking the sea. There is also an entertainment lounge and separate bar area. Offers ferry discounts too. £

THE HAVELOCK MAP P.58. 2 Queen's Rd, PO37 6AN. http://havelockhotel.co.uk. A range of 19 stylish, modern rooms here at this clifftop hotel, which also boasts a Mediterranean-esque outdoor pool (heated), well-clipped gardens and free parking. Some rooms have balconies. Three-night minimum stay. £££

HAVEN HALL HOTEL MAP P.58. 5 Howard Rd, PO37 6HD. https://www. havenhallhotel.com/. This sprawling clifftop house in Shanklin features 17 rooms, with three on the ground floor and seven available for self-catering. Nearly every room overlooks the water and there are landscaped gardens, a swimming pool and a grass tennis court. The dreamy rooms are spacious and feature period pieces, as well as marble bathrooms. £££

LUCCOMBE HALL MAP P.58. Luccombe Rd, PO37 6RL. http://luccombehall.co.uk. This sprawling country house, set amongst four acres of gardens, has amazing views from its clifftop position down over Shanklin beach and the Solent beyond, which you can admire from its gardens, windowed terrace or (some) rooms. Choose from standard, sea-facing, family or even one with its own private hot tub, among other room types. Facilities include indoor and outdoor children's play areas, heated swimming pools, a games room and even a mini putting green. Offers ferry discount deals. £££

RYLSTONE MANOR MAP P.58. Rylstone Gardens, PO37 6RG. http://rylstone-manor. co.uk. Each room is named after a different tree, and as such are individually styled while retaining the overall style of this Victorian house. That's not the only thing that makes it a quaint place to stay, though, as it's nestled in the heart of the leafy Rylstone Gardens. ££

Ventnor to Blackgang

APPULDURCOMBE GARDENS HOLIDAY PARK MAP P.66. Wroxall, PO38 3EP. http://appuldurcombegardens.co.uk. This award-winning holiday park is set amongst 14 acres of secluded grounds with the open countryside beyond – and just three miles from Shanklin and Ventnor. Part of the island's Area of Outstanding Natural Beauty, this is a fab spot for those looking for walks, cycles and birdwatching; as for the campsite itself, the on-site facilities can complement your stay. There's a range of accommodation options, including lodges, motorhomes, static camping and apartments. Rates vary depending on accommodation type.

ENCHANTED MANOR MAP P.66. Sandrock Rd, PO38 2NG. http://enchantedmanor.co.uk. Fairy-themed guesthouse in Niton with eight extravagant suites, complete with fairy-tale décor and artworks. It's certainly a unique spot for a romantic stay; there's also a billiard room, games room and bar. Two-night minimum stay. ££

THE HAMBROUGH MAP P.66. Hambrough Rd, Ventnor, PO38 1SQ. http://thehambrough.com. Seven slick, simple rooms all with seaviews (bar one) spread across two floors. A great place to relax, unwind and take part in nearby coastal activities, from walks and sailing to horse-riding and sunbathing. They also run three self-catering properties: Quince Cottage, Villa Lavinia and Villa Apartment. Dine at their on-site restaurant. ££

NETTLECOMBE FARM HOLIDAY COTTAGES MAP P.66 Whitwell, PO38 2AF. http://www.nettlecombefarm.co.uk/. Choose from nine dog-friendly self-catering cottages at this award-winning accommodation nestled in the countryside, just outside Ventnor. The converted barns, stables, farmhouses and cottages sleep between three–ten guests, but only the two cottages include Wi-Fi, with an extra charge applicable for the others. Available by the week. £££

ROYAL HOTEL MAP P.66. Belgrave Rd, Ventnor, PO38 1JJ. http://royalhoteliow.co.uk. The clue is in the name with this sprawling 51-bedroomed complex, one of the island's oldest hotels built in 1832. The hotel is far from stuck in the past, with elegantly styled rooms mixing classic and contemporary in just the right amounts. Make sure you enjoy breakfast in the conservatory or dinner in the plush restaurant. One accessible room. £££

THE TERRACE ROOMS & WINE MAP P.66 The Cascades, Ventnor, PO38 1TA. https://www.theterraceventnor.co.uk/. Live the life of luxury at this boutique guesthouse, with five double rooms and a dog-friendly annexe room. All rooms have seaviews, super-king beds and White Company linen. Even more temptingly, their rates include an evening wine tasting. £££

Brighstone to Alum Bay

COMPTON FARM MAP P.76. Brook, PO30 4HF. http://comptonfarm.co.uk. This basic campsite is set on a level field surrounded by an 18-acre wildflower meadow, and is within easy walking distance from the beach. Showers cost extra but all other facilities are included (toilets, laundry room, washing up stations). Rates vary depending on accommodation type.

FARRINGFORD MAP P.76. Bedbury Lane, PO40 9PE. https://farringford.co.uk/. Choose from five self-catering cottages which sleep two–eight guests. Their Alfred Cottages are charmingly cute with blue-panelled exterior, high ceilings and fitted woodburners (logs provided), while the bricked Stable Cottages span two floors and include their own courtyard. Two-night minimum stay. £££

GRANGE FARM MAP P.76. Military Rd, PO30 4DA. http://grangefarmholidays.com. Choose from campsites (traditional to electrical hook-ups), static caravans or cottages here at this family-run farm, spread across 60 acres of land. Overlooking Brighstone Bay, the site also includes a playground, a facilities block (free showers, washing machines, baby-changing areas) and a reception-shop for food essentials (including ice cream). Rates vary depending on accommodation type.

TOM'S ECO LODGE MAP P.76. Tapnell Farm, Newport Rd, PO41 0YJ. http://tomsecolodge.com. There's a range of quirky glamping options here, from safari tents and wooden cabins to eco pods and modulogs (cabins designed exclusively for Tom's Eco Lodge). They can all be rented on Tapnell Farm, an area that offers privacy and seaviews all rolled into one. Rates vary depending on accommodation type.

Yarmouth and around

THE BUGLE COACHING INN MAP P.87. The Square, PO41 0NS. www.characterinns.co.uk/the-bugle-coaching-inn. This 16th-century coaching inn is best known for its hearty grub, but that should be good enough reason to stay over as well, right? Upstairs are seven en-suite rooms – some with views overlooking the Market Square – with wooden furniture and blue decor. £

CALBORNE WATER MILL MAP P.84. Westover, Calbourne, PO30 4JN. http://calbournewatermill.co.uk. Within the mill complex, you can take your pick from luxury eco-friendly lodges, traditional cottages and a camping and caravan park. As well as being close to a fenced stream, roaming peacocks and overlooking the peaceful woodland, there's also an on-site café that serves up delicious Sunday lunches. £

THE GEORGE HOTEL MAP P.87. Quay St, PO41 0PE. http://thegeorge.co.uk. This seventeenth-century townhouse, squeezed in between Yarmouth Castle and the pier, sits on the water's edge and isn't far from the ferry terminal. The rooms are lavishly decorated to the perfect amount, and there's a fantastic restaurant on site, too. One accessible room on the ground floor. £££

JIREH HOUSE MAP P.87. St James' Square, PO41 0NP. www.jireh-house.com. This seventeenth-century cottage is a cosy fit of six rooms, three of which share bathroom facilities. It retains a traditional character throughout, and rooms include a small television and hot drinks facilities. There's a popular teahouse downstairs, where guests can enjoy breakfast from, and is usually bustling all afternoon until the close of day. £

THE ORCHARDS HOLIDAY PARK MAP P.84. Main Rd, Newbridge, PO41 0TS. http://orchards-holiday-park.co.uk. Just over four miles southeast of Yarmouth is this family-owned holiday park, where you can rent caravans or bring your own, as well as camping pitches. For something sturdier, check into their stone-built Orchard House, complete with its own patio and garden area. There are dog-walking and recreational areas, indoor and outdoor pools, table tennis and a facilities centre. Rates vary depending on accommodation type.

ESSENTIALS

Crossing the water on a hovercraft

Arrival

Make your entrance to the Isle of Wight from a choice of ferries, catamarans or hovercraft. Whichever way you choose, as you approach the island across the Solent (the strait between the mainland and the island), you'll pass by plenty of sailing yachts and speedboats zigzagging across the waves also en route to the island or further afield. From London, it takes around three hours by car or just over two and a half hours by public transport, with three well-connected mainland points (Portsmouth, Southampton and Lymington) to make the final leg of the journey across from.

By ferry

There are three departure points from the mainland: Portsmouth, Southampton and Lymington. Fare structures and schedules on all routes are labyrinthine, so check the companies' websites for full details of current fares and schedules.

From **Portsmouth**, Wightlink runs car ferries from the Gunwharf Terminal to Fishbourne (takes 45min), and a high-speed FastCat catamaran from Portsmouth Harbour to Ryde Pier Head (foot passengers only; takes 22min).

Lymington offers the fastest car ferry route (40min) with Wightlink car ferries (03339 997333, http://wightlink.co.uk) to Yarmouth.

Red Funnel operates a high-speed catamaran from **Southampton** to West Cowes (foot passengers only; takes 28min) and one with cars to East Cowes (takes 1hr). You can jump on the free shuttle bus service from Southampton Central train station to the ferry terminal.

These timetables may vary slightly by season; check the relevant websites for details.

By hovercraft

Hovertravel (03452 220461, http://hovertravel.co.uk) runs hovercrafts from Clarence Esplanade in Southsea to Ryde (foot passengers only; every 30min; Portsmouth–Ryde typically Mon–Fri 6.30am–8.30pm, Sat 8am–8.30pm, Sun 8.30am–8.30pm, Ryde–Portsmouth typically Mon–Fri 6.15am–8.15pm, Sat 7.45am–8.15pm, Sun 8.15am–8.15pm; 10min). This is certainly the most unique way to reach the island, being the world's only commercial passenger hovercraft service. Bumping along the waves on one of these 'flights' is a unique way to make your entrance to the island, and you can take light luggage on board with you. The hovercraft pulls up along the Esplanade, next to the bus station, but note the timetable can be affected when there are adverse weather conditions.

By air

There are two small airfields on the Isle of Wight: Bembridge Airport

Travelling to the Isle of Wight

Lymington to Yarmouth: **Wightlink** 03339 997333, http://wightlink.co.uk.

Portsmouth to Fishbourne or Ryde: **Wightlink** 03339 997333, http://wightlink.co.uk.

Southampton to Cowes: **Red Funnel** 02380 019192, http://redfunnel.co.uk.

Southsea to Ryde: **Hovertravel** 03452 220461, http://hovertravel.co.uk.

(http://eghj.extremelynice.net/eghj) and Sandown Airport (http://eghn.org.uk), but these are for private planes only. If you're coming from further afield, you'll need to fly into one of the mainland airports (Bournemouth and Southampton closest) and make your way down by car or train to one of the ports listed in this chapter.

By public transport
Visitors can travel with **National Express** (08717 818181, http://nationalexpress.com) with prices varying depending on your starting location and cheaper if booked in advance. For example, from London Victoria Coach Station to Portsmouth (the Hard terminal for the ferries or Southsea for the Hovercraft) costs around £20–30 for a return journey and takes roughly two hours each way.

Alternatively, there are frequent trains from the likes of London Waterloo and London Victoria to **Portsmouth Harbour** and **Southampton Central**. Return journeys cost around £50 – again, cheaper if booked in advance – and takes one to three hours each way.

Getting around

With efficient and (mostly) modern public transport available, it's easy enough to get around the island without a car. Buses are fairly frequent and there are free timetables you can pick up at stations and visitor information points, which give detailed instructions on bus and train routes, as well as helpful timetables. There aren't any motorways on the Isle of Wight, just country roads and main roads, but everywhere is well signposted and easy to navigate, making it an ideal destination for keen walkers and cyclists.

Buses
Local buses are run by **Southern Vectis** (01983 827000, http://islandbuses.info), who sell good-value tickets offering unlimited travel across their network. The modern buses are bright green, single- and double-decker and include USB charging points. For unlimited bus travel for 24 hours, opt for Day Rover tickets (adults £10, ages 5–16 £6, groups up to five £27.50), while Rover+Breezer tickets are available for 24 or 48 hour travel (£14/£17.50, ages 17–18 £11/£13.50, ages 5–16 £7.50/£9.50, groups up to five £35/£42). Multi-day ticket bundles and their

Take a day out on a bus tour
Southern Vectis run four hop-on, hop-off bus tours during the summer season. These open- or closed-top tourist buses run daily and may include commentaries about the sights and attractions you pass by. See below for individual routes and operating months.

The **Downs Breezer** runs between Ryde and Bembridge via Sandown (daily May–Oct); the **Island Coaster** runs between Ryde and Alum Bay via Shanklin, Ventnor and Blackgang (daily April–Sept); the **Needles Breezer** runs between Alum Bay and Needles Battery via Yarmouth (daily March to Sept); the **Shanklin Shuttle** covers the Chine, Old Village, main town and beachfront Esplanade (daily May–Sept); and the **Summer Links** runs between Newport and Yarmouth via Calbourne Water Mill (daily April–Oct).

Freedom Tickets are good value for longer stays; choose from 5, 15 or 30 days with multi-day ticket bundles (adults from £31) or 7, 30 or 90 days with Freedom Tickets (adults from £28).

Tickets can be bought via their mobile app, their Travel Shops or direct from the driver. Some hotels even offer free or discounted bus passes for guests.

Bus routes

Bus #1 Newport to Cowes; bus #2 Newport to Ryde via Merstone; bus #3 Newport to Ryde via Rookley; bus #4 Ryde to East Cowes; bus #5 Newport to East Cowes; bus #6 Newport to Ventnor; bus #7 Newport to Alum Bay via Yarmouth; bus #8 Newport to Ryde via Amazon World and Bembridge; bus #9 Newport to Ryde via Medina; bus #12 Newport to Alum Bay via Freshwater Bay; bus #22 Shanklin town service; bus #24 Yaverland to Shanklin; bus #32 Cowes to Northwood circular via Gurnard; bus #37 Ryde town service; bus #38 Newport town service.

Most run half-hourly or hourly; check the website for individual and up-to-date timetables.

Trains

There are two rail lines on the island. The **Island Line** (http://southwesternrailway.com) spans 8.5-miles and runs from Ryde Pier to Shanklin, serving Smallbrook Junction, Brading, Sandown and Lake stations. Rather uniquely, the trains are made up of former London Underground carriages; in 2021, five Class 484 trains replaced their 82-year-old Class 483 trains. The refurbished rolling stock now includes upgraded interiors, plug sockets, USB

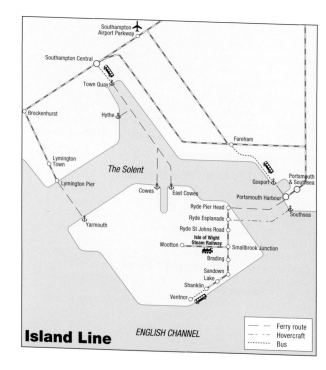

charging points, wheelchair spaces and free Wi-Fi.

The second rail line is the **Isle of Wight Steam Railway** (http://iwsteamrailway.co.uk) which runs to and from Havenstreet via Smallbrook Junction and Wootton (4-9 daily) and you can alight at Smallbrook Junction for Island Line services to Ryde and Shanklin.

Cycling

Cycling is a popular way of getting around the island; ferries, catamarans and the hovercraft all accept bikes on board. There's the 65-mile Round the Island route, which is well-signposted (white signs with a blue island means clockwise, blue signs with a white island anti-clockwise). In the summer, the narrow lanes can get very busy, but stopping off at small towns along the way helps break the journey up.

If you're looking to rent a bike, there are plenty of options. Check out **Wight Cycle Hire** in Yarmouth (£14/half-day, £20/day; 01983 761800, http://wightcyclehire.co.uk); **TAV Cycles** in Ryde (£12/half-day, £18/day, 01983 812989, https://tavcycles.co.uk/); **South Island Cycle Hire** in Cowes (£14/half-day, £20/day; 01983 755007, https://www.southislandcyclehire.co.uk/); and **Routetfifty7** in Shanklin (£15/half-day, £20/day; 07491 000057, http://routefifty7.com), amongst many more. Most of these have multi-day options and they can collect and deliver bikes across the island.

Some would argue that cycling is the best way to experience the Isle of Wight: routes will see you take in a variety of landscapes, from fantastic stretches of coastline and narrow country roads to dense woodland and pretty estuaries.

Walking

The majority of the island is a designated Area of Outstanding Natural Beauty and is a very popular destination for walkers and hikers, with a variety of gradients to choose from. The coastal, public footpath around the island covers roughly 70 miles, which experienced walkers could complete in as little as four days, although this is one of the more challenging options. There are various walking guides available in bookstores such as *Medina* in Cowes (see page 32), and plenty of resources online, too.

The island is quite hilly, which is something to bear in mind if you're trying to track down a hotel with a suitcase in tow, and huge buses weave through steep, narrow roads, so always mind where you're going. It's important to wear appropriate footwear, particularly if you're covering some of the hilly headlands.

Driving

Although driving is the most straight-forward way to get around the island, the Isle of Wight supports a number of local sustainability schemes to encourage drivers to leave their car at home. This is within reason, of course, and there are still many conveniently placed car parks dotted around the island. Some hotels provide free parking to guests, a few sights offer discounted entry to visitors who have reached them by 'sustainable methods' (by foot, bike or public transport) and there are four electric car charge points for electric vehicles.

That said, the lack of motorways on the island means that there are some lovely, scenic routes past large stretches of countryside and horizon-lined coastal views: worth navigating are Middle Road from Newport to Freshwater, and Military Road from Freshwater to Chale.

To find out more about renting a car on the island, head to http://visitisleofwight.co.uk/travel/getting-around/by-car.

Boat trips

Flanked by the Solent and English Channel, guided boat trips and pleasure cruises are a great way to take in the surroundings of the island by water. Needles Pleasure Cruises offer 'slow' and 'fast' cruises from five various-sized boats (01983 761587, www.needlespleasurecruises. co.uk/the-trips); board at the end of the pier on Alum Bay. Trips vary in length of time depending on the tide and type of boat, with routes covering Yarmouth, The Needles and Scratchells Bay.

There's also **Coral Star** (01983 760212, https://www.facebook.com/ thecoralstar), a blue, wooden boat providing running commentaries between routes from Yarmouth to Lymington on the mainland (4 daily), plus trips to see the Needles (Mon, Wed, Fri and Sun, weather permitting).

Directory A–Z

Accessible travel

There are plenty of disabled car parking spaces on the Isle of Wight, and buses accommodate wheelchairs and mobility scooters. The Island Line train service is also accessible.

All ferry and hovercraft options request 48hr notice before travelling if you are disabled; a blue badge is required by marine law.

For general planning tips and other useful resources, you can find out more on **Motability** (www.motability. co.uk).

Children

The island is great fun for children of all ages, with long stretches of beaches, themed amusement parks and plenty of watersports to get stuck into.

Most pubs and restaurants are family-friendly, and some have family rooms or beer gardens where children are welcome. While plenty offer family rooms, some B&Bs and hotels don't accept children under a certain age (usually 12), but there's plenty of self-catering accommodation for however many are in your group – it can be easier (and more fun) for kids, too.

Many public museums and attractions have kids' activity packs, family events, play areas and more, and you can find a playground or park in most neighbourhoods. Children (usually under 16s) are usually entitled to concessionary rates across many attractions, and under-5s generally travel free on public transport.

Cinema

There are just two cinemas on the Isle of Wight: a **Cineworld** in Newport (Coppins Bridge, PO30 2TA; www. cineworld.co.uk/cinemas/newport-isle-of-wight) and **Commodore** in Ryde (2 Star St, PO33 2HX; http:// leoleisurecommodore.co.uk/ryde/now). Both are multi-screened and show the latest blockbusters.

Over the summer months, a range of outdoor cinema screenings take place across some lovely locations, such as **Puckpool Park** in Seaview, **Mottistone Gardens** in Newport and **Ventnor Botanic Gardens**. **The Garlic Farm** (see page 39) screens cult classics and family-friendly films (usually over the Bank Holiday weekends) on-site where guests can tuck into barbecue food and purchase hot and cold drinks from the restaurant; tickets are usually around £8.

There's also the **Isle of Wight Film Festival**, part of the **Ventnor Fringe Festival** (see page 65), which screens classic and independent films throughout the year – check out http:// vfringe.co.uk for more information.

Crime and emergencies

The Isle of Wight does not see a lot of crime and visitors will feel safe in most areas, but as with most places, it's still important to act sensibly and report anything that doesn't look right.

The emergency numbers for the Police, Fire Brigade, Ambulance and Coastguard are 999, or 101 for non-emergencies.

Discount passes

Many of the island's historic attractions – from castles to stately homes – are owned and/or operated by either the National Trust (http:// nationaltrust.org.uk) and English Heritage (http://english-heritage. org.uk). They usually charge entry fees, though most sites are free for members.

A few hotels on the island offer free bus passes, while other hotels provide discounts for island-crossing travel if you book directly with them. There are a range of combination-package deals (ie transport and accommodation) covered in one price, which can be worth taking advantage of depending on the length of the trip or simply to save you some time.

More and more attractions are beginning to offer discounted entry if you arrive to their site by sustainable transport (walking, cycling or public transport).

Electricity

The current is 240V AC. North American appliances will need a transformer and adaptor; those from Europe, South Africa, Australia and New Zealand only need an adaptor.

Health

There is one hospital on the Isle of Wight, in Newport (St Mary's Hospital Parkhurst Rd, PO30 5TG; 01983 822099, http://iow.nhs.uk). There are medical centres and pharmacies across the island, in both main towns and surrounding areas. The Isle of Wight NHS website provides an extensive list of every pharmacy on the island including their address, website and telephone number ((https://www.iow.nhs.uk/contact-us/ useful-numbers-and-addresses/isle-of-wight-pharmacies.htm).

Internet

Free wi-fi is available in most places, although the speed varies depending where you are – you're less likely to have a strong connection on Tennyson Down compared to Newport's high street, for instance. Some of the older hotels and sights out in the sticks might not have fast connections as their number one priority. It's best to take printed copies of timetables and maps with you – and this guidebook, of course – where you don't need to rely on signal to navigate your way around, particularly if you're cycling or hiking.

Left luggage

There aren't any official luggage storage points on the island, nor can you store anything at the ferry ports, either. Most hotels and other accommodation types should be able to hold onto your luggage for you, but it is worth checking directly with the hotel at the time of booking. There are some independent services who will move your luggage around for you, such as Move My Bag (www. movemybag-isleofwight.co.uk), which can come in very handy if you are cycling or walking from point to point.

LGBTQ travellers

The Isle of Wight and England itself are generally tolerant places for the LGBTQ community. There's an annual LGBTQ

Public holidays

Britain's public holidays (Bank Holidays), are:

January 1
Good Friday
Easter Monday
First Monday in May
Last Monday in May
Last Monday in August
December 25
December 26

Note that if January 1, December 25 or December 26 falls on a Saturday or Sunday, the next weekday becomes a public holiday.

Pride which takes place in Ryde (www. iwpride.org).

Lost property

Lost property (or anything found) should be reported on the Hampshire Police website here: www.hampshire. police.uk/ro/report/lp/lost-or-found- property.

Maps

The Ordnance Survey (OS) produces the most comprehensive and detailed maps, renowned for their accuracy and clarity. Planning on going hiking or following simple trails? Then these are a must. Their 1:50,000 (pink) Landranger series shows enough detail to be useful for most walkers and cyclists, and there's more detail still in the full-colour 1:25,000 (orange) Explorer series. Both also have mobile versions available.

There's also a range of walking maps available in bookstores and online, and a selection at the Medina bookstore in West Cowes (see page 32).

If you only require a general route overview, however, there are various road atlases also available, at a scale of around 1:250,000.

Money (ATMs, banks, costs, credit cards, exchange)

Britain's currency is the pound sterling (£), divided into 100 pence (p). Coins come in denominations of 1p, 2p, 5p, 10p, 20p, 50p, £1 and £2. Notes are in denominations of £5, £10, £20 and £50. Scottish and Northern Irish banknotes are legal tender throughout Britain, though some traders may be unwilling to accept them. Some places accept euros. For current exchange rates, visit http://xe.com.

Opening hours

Though traditional business hours are Monday to Saturday from around 9am to 5.30/6pm, most shops and supermarkets open earlier, close later and larger chains usually stay open on Sundays. Banks are closed at the weekends, but a few branches open on Saturday mornings. Smaller villages and more remote areas might have a tendency to do their own thing – but that's part of the charm.

Outside of the summer, a few places shut up shop for the off-season, but most of the major attractions stay open year-round (with the Christmas period a flexible exception). You might find that a number of restaurants and cafes close between lunch and dinner (typically 3–5pm).

Post offices

Pretty much every single post office is open Monday to Friday between 9am to 5.30pm, and until 1pm on Saturdays; some smaller branches are closed on Wednesday afternoons. Stamps can be bought here, but also from newsagents, many gift shops and supermarkets.

To find out your nearest post office, see http://postoffice.co.uk.

Smoking

Smoking is banned in all public buildings and offices, restaurants and pubs, and on all public transport. Vaping – the use of e-cigarettes – is not allowed on public transport and is generally prohibited in museums and other public buildings; for restaurants and bars it depends on the individual proprietor, who will sometimes display a sign to note if it's permitted or not.

Time

Greenwich Mean Time (GMT) – equivalent to Coordinated Universal Time (UTC) – is used from the end of October to the end of March; for the rest of the year Britain switches to British Summer Time (BST), one hour ahead of GMT. GMT is five hours ahead of the US Eastern Standard Time and ten hours behind Australian Eastern Standard Time.

Tipping

Although there are no fixed rules for tipping, a ten to fifteen percent tip is anticipated by restaurant waiters, as in the rest of the UK. Some restaurants may levy a "discretionary" or "optional" service charge of 10 or 12.5 percent. If they've done this, it should be clearly stated on the menu and on the bill. However, you are not obliged to pay the charge, and certainly not if the food or service wasn't what you expected. Cafés and bars may also leave a jar at the bar for small tips.

Toilets

There are public toilets available across the island, bus stations to wilder outposts; some are free, others incur a small charge.

Tourist information

There are 13 tourist information points on the Isle of Wight; see www.visitisleofwight.co.uk/travel/tourist-information-points for details:
Bembridge
Brading
Brighstone
Cowes
East Cowes
Freshwater Bay
Godshill
Havenstreet
Newport (Newport Bus Station and Quay Arts Centre)
Ryde
Sandown

Price codes

The below prices for eating throughout the book are based on a meal for one with a non-alcoholic drink:

£	under £20
££	£20-30
£££	£31-45
££££	over £45

The below prices for accommodation (see page 102) are based on a double room, including breakfast, unless otherwise stated:

£	under £100
££	£100-199
£££	over £200

Ventnor
Yarmouth

Many places (hotels, museums, main bus stations) provide a selection of free brochures detailing different attractions around the island; hotel/B&B owners are usually happy to help; and some self-catering accommodation may provide information packs. If in doubt, the official island website, http://visitisleofwight.co.uk, has extensive coverage of the Isle of Wight, as does http://isleofwight.com.

Festivals and events

The iconic Isle of Wight Festival found its roots in 1968, but after the infamous 1970 festival, it was banned until 2002. The island is renowned for its sailing events, including the world-famous Cowes Week. There are plenty of carnivals, fayres and markets that promote the best the island has to offer locals and visitors of all ages. Here are some of the best, listed below.

Walk the Wight

May and October, http://isleofwightwalkingfestival.co.uk. The UK's longest-running and largest walking festival, including a cross-island trek for those who are up for something a bit extra. There are different walks to take that sees walkers covering sand dunes and quiet coves to bustling sailing towns and sleepy villages.

Isle of Wight Festival

June, http://isleofwightfestival.com. Annual festival that attracts major names, from Blondie and Jimi Hendrix to the Foo Fighters and Amy Winehouse. This is the biggest festival on the island and is one of the best-known across the entire country for its mix of music.

Round the Island Race

July, www.roundtheisland.org.uk. This is your chance to see some of the world's best sailors tackle the Round the Island Race, which starts and finishes at Cowes. This one-day event attracts over 1400 boats and around 15,000 sailors, and there are numerous vantage points to get a good view.

Sandown Carnival

July, http://sandowncarnival.com. The Sandown Carnival has been running since 1889, filled with marching bands, lively parades, numerous events and fireworks at the island's south-coast resort.

Ventnor Fringe Festival

July, http://vfringe.co.uk. Make the most of the island's vibrant arts and culture centre at this six-day festival, including theatre, comedy, cabaret and musical performances.

Cowes Week

July/August, http://aamcowesweek.co.uk. One of the world's largest and much looked forward to sailing events, Cowes Week has been a key highlight in the British sporting calendar since it started in 1826. Olympic, world-class and weekend yachtsmen take part (in nearly 1000 boats) in different races over eight days.

The Wight Proms

August, www.wightproms.co.uk. Held at Northwood Park in Cowes, the hugely popular Proms features comedy nights, classical performances, an outdoor cinema and free theatre workshops over the space of at least seven days.

Garlic Festival

August, http://garlicfestival.co.uk. This family-friendly festival offers live music, food stalls and a fun atmosphere. It's one of the largest and most popular events on the island – and of course, there's no better place to sample local garlic.

Island Steam Fair

August, http://iwsteamrailway.co.uk. Variety of displays and attractions, with comedy and entertainment arenas, live music, traditional fairground rides and working steam train demonstrations. There's also a range of vintage cars and old wagons, or hop on board for a classic steam train ride through the countryside.

International Charity Classic Car Show

September, https://www.facebook. com/iowclassiccarshow. A fantastic range of vintage, classic, custom and retro cars descend to the island over a weekend, first parking at Newport Harbour before going on display in Ryde.

Isle of Wight Literary Festival

October, https:// isleofwightliteraryfestival.com. This is your chance to step inside Northwood House, where you can listen to a range of talks – previous speakers include Alan Titchmarsh, Dr Maggie Aderin-Pocock and Jo Brand – covering a fascinating array of topics.

Chronology

7000–6000 BC Isle of Wight forms as an island

43 AD Roman conquest of Britain, including Isle of Wight

280 Newport Roman Villa built

530 Saxons defeat Bowcombe Valley natives (near Newport) and takes island

686 Island is the last part of England to be converted to Christianity

1066 William Fitz Osbern is the first Lord of the island

1262 Isabella de Fortibus inherits Carisbrooke Castle

1362 English becomes the country's official language, taking over from French

1445 Henry Beauchamp crowned King of the Wight

1535 King Henry VIII instructs major fortification of island coastline

1545 Last French invasion

1582–84 Bubonic plague hits Newport

1584 Majority of pirates in the country are believed to be between Isle of Wight and Poole

1648 King Charles tries to escape from Carisbrooke Castle

1700 Bembridge Windmill built; Cowes shipbuilding yards established

1814 Ryde Pier opens

1827 The artist Turner paints while a guest at East Cowes Castle

1831 Twelve-year-old future Queen Victoria stays at Norris Castle

1833 Royal Yacht Squadron founded at Cowes

1843 Blackgang Chine opens

1845 Prince Albert acquires Osborne House for Queen Victoria

1864 Julia Margaret Cameron takes first photographs at Dimbola Lodge

1901 Queen Victoria dies at Osborne House, aged 81

1942 Polish Destroyer ship Blyskawica defends Cowes in Second World War

1956–71 Secret rocket testing near Freshwater Bay

1968 First Isle of Wight Festival

1970 Legendary Isle of Wight Festival attracts 600,000 hippies; this is the last one until 2002

1980 Isle of Wight International Scooter Rally launches

1995 Island restructures from two borough councils to one Isle of Wight Council

1999 First all-ladies crew row around the island, in 10 hours and 20 minutes

2002 The Isle of Wight Festival is reinstated

2004 Cowes Hammerhead Crane becomes Grade II listed

2019 Isle of Wight receives UNESCO Biosphere Reserve status

2023 Wet Leg, an indie-rock band from the Isle of Wight, scoop an impressive four awards at the 2023 BRIT Awards.

Publishing Information
Second edition 2023

Distribution
UK, Ireland and Europe
Apa Publications (UK) Ltd; sales@roughguides.com
United States and Canada
Ingram Publisher Services; ips@ingramcontent.com
Australia and New Zealand
Booktopia; retailer@booktopia.com.au
Worldwide
Apa Publications (UK) Ltd; sales@roughguides.com

Special Sales, Content Licensing and CoPublishing
Rough Guides can be purchased in bulk quantities at discounted prices. We can
create special editions, personalised jackets and corporate imprints tailored to
your needs. sales@roughguides.com.
roughguides.com

Printed in China
This book was produced using **Typefi** automated publishing software.

A catalogue record for this book is available from the British Library
The publishers and authors have done their best to ensure the accuracy
and currency of all the information in **Pocket Rough Guide Isle of
Wight**, however, they can accept no responsibility for any loss, injury, or
inconvenience sustained by any traveller as a result of information or advice
contained in the guide.

Rough Guide Credits
Editor: Sarah Clark
Cartography: Katie Bennett
Picture editor: Tom Smyth
Layout: Grzegorz Madejak

Original design: Richard Czapnik
Head of DTP and Pre-Press:
Rebeka Davies
Head of Publishing: Sarah Clark

About the author
Aimee White is a freelance travel writer based in Portsmouth. She was
previously the Senior Features Writer at loveEXPLORING.com and Senior Editor
at Rough Guides, and also hosted *The Rough Guide to Everywhere* travel
podcast. Find out more at aimeewhite.uk.

Acknowledgements

Aimee would like to thank Simon Clark at Visit Isle of Wight and Loretta Lale at Hovertravel for all their help and assistance. Many thanks also to Sarah Clark for the commission, Katie Bennett for her magical map skills and the rest of the team at Rough Guides for their support.

Help us update

We've gone to a lot of effort to ensure that this edition of the **Pocket Rough Guide Isle of Wight** is accurate and up-to-date. However, things change – places get "discovered", opening hours are notoriously fickle, restaurants and rooms raise prices or lower standards. If you feel we've got it wrong or left something out, we'd like to know, and if you can remember the address, the price, the hours, the phone number, so much the better.

Please send your comments with the subject line "**Pocket Rough Guide Isle of Wight Update**" to mail@uk.roughguides.com. We'll credit all contributions and send a copy of the next edition (or any other Rough Guide if you prefer) for the very best emails.

Photo Credits

(Key: T-top; C-centre; B-bottom; L-left; R-right)

Alamy 12T, 16T, 26, 27, 34, 71, 73, 88

Amanda Wheeler/The Crab Shed 72

Boynton and Jones Photography/ Heron 48

Diana Jarvis/Rough Guides 33, 38

Eileen Long Photography/Inns of Distinction 55

English Heritage 23TC

iStock 6, 12B, 14T, 15B, 15T, 17T, 18C, 19T, 20T, 44, 47, 51, 52, 56, 89

N.Cayla on Wikimedia Commons 59

Portsmouth City Council 96

Shutterstock 4, 5, 10, 11T, 11B, 13, 18T, 19C, 20C, 20B, 21T, 21B, 22T, 22C, 22B, 23B, 29, 31, 35, 39, 42, 49, 60, 61, 63, 66, 68, 70, 74, 82, 87, 90, 91, 92, 93, 94, 95, 97, 98, 99, 108/109

Slab Artisan Fudge 32

User Nilfanion at Wikimedia Commons 23C

Vectis Ventures 41

www.visitisleofwight.co.uk 1, 2T, 2BL, 2C, 2BR, 13, 14B, 16B, 17B, 18C, 19C, 21C, 25, 37, 40, 43, 62, 64, 65, 75, 77, 78, 80, 81, 83, 84, 86, 100/101

Cover: The Needles **Shutterstock**

Index

A

accessible travel 114
accommodation 102
  Albert Cottage 102
  Appuldurcombe Gardens
    Holiday Park 105
  Aqua Hotel 105
  Busigny House 102
  Calborne Water Mill 107
  Calverts 103
  Compton Farm 106
  Duke of York 102
  Enchanted Manor 106
  Farringford 106
  Foresters Hall 102
  Grange Farm 106
  Harold House 102
  Haven Hall Hotel 105
  Hewitt's House 103
  Holly Tree House 103
  Into the Woods 103
  Jireh House 107
  Luccombe Hall 105
  Nettlecombe Farm Holiday
    Cottages 106
  New Holmwood Hotel 103
  Nodes Point Holiday Park
    104
  Northbank Hotel 104
  One Holyrood B&B 103
  Pilot Boat Inn 105
  Royal Esplanade 104
  Royal Hotel 106
  Ryde Castle 104
  Rylstone Manor 105
  Sorrento Lodge 104
  TEXAS American School Bus
    Glamping 104
  The Bugle Coaching Inn 107
  The George Hotel 107
  The Hambrough 106
  The Little Gloster 103
  The Orchards Holiday Park 107
  The Seaview 105
  The Terrace Rooms &
    Wine 106
  Tom's Eco Lodge 106
  Union Inn 103
  Villa Rothsay 103
  Wheatsheaf 104
  Yelf's 104
Adgestone Vineyard 52
Alum Bay 78
Amazon World 60
Appley to Seagrove Bay
  walk 46
Appuldurcombe House 68
arrival 110

B

Bembridge 51
Bembridge Fort and Downs 53
Bembridge Windmill 52
Blackgang Chine 69
boat trips 114
Bonchurch 67
Botanical Gardens 65
Brading Roman Villa 52
Brighstone 74
Brighstone Museum 75
Brighstone to Alum Bay 74
buses 111
bus tours 111
Butterfly World 41
by air 110
by ferry 110
by hovercraft 110
by public transport 111

C

cafés
  Baywatch on the Beach Café 54
  Bluebells Café 42
  Caffè Isola 42
  Cantina Ventnor 71
  Castlehaven Beach Cafe 72
  Chocolate Apothecary 49
  ComiCoffee 43
  Dell Café 54
  Eegon's of Cowes 34
  God's Providence House 43
  Jolliffe's 34
  Lily's 55
  No64 49
  Old Thatch Teashop 62
  Piano Café 80
  PO41 89
  Sails of Cowes 35
  Smugglers' Haven Tea
    Gardens 72
  Sounds + Grounds 35
  Tansy's Pantry 72
  The Blue Door 42
  The Crab Shed 72
  The Gaslight 62
  The Gossips Café 89
  The Reef 63
cafés (by area)
  Brighstone to Alum Bay 80
  Cowes and around 34
  Newport and around 42
  Ryde and around 49
  The east coast 54
  The south coast 62
  Ventnor to Blackgang 71
  Yarmouth and around 89

Calbourne Water Mill 86
Carisbrooke CastleCastle 37
children 114
chronology 119
cinema 114
Classic Boat Museum 27
Coastal trail, Colwell Bay to
  Totland Bay 75
Compton Bay 79
Cowes Maritime Museum 27
Cowes Week 29
crime and emergencies 115
cycling 113

D

Devil's Chimney 67
Dimbola Lodge 76
Dinosaur Capital of Britain 57
Dinosaur Isle 59
directory A-Z 114
discount passes 115
drinking 7
driving 113

E

East Cowes Heritage Centre 28
eating 7
electricity 115
entertainment
  Quay Arts 43
entertainment (by area)
  Newport and around 43

F

Farringford 75
festivals and events 118
  Cowes Week 118
  Garlic Festival 119
  International Charity Classic Car
    Show 119
  Island Steam Show 119
  Isle of Wight Festival 118
  Isle of Wight Literary Festival
    119
  Round the Island Race 118
  Sandown Carnival 118
  The Wight Proms 118
  Ventnor Fringe Festival 118
  Walk the Wight 117
Fort Victoria Country Park 83

G

getting around 111
Godshill 68

INDEX

Godshill Model Village 69
going out 7
Goodleaf Tree Climbing 45
Gurnard Bay 31

H

Haven Falconry 45
health 115
Horseshoe Bay 53

I

International scooter rally 47
internet 115
Isle of Wight Distillery 51
Isle of Wight Donkey Sanctuary 68
Isle of Wight Steam Railway 40
itineraries 18

L

left luggage 115
LGBTQ travellers 115
link to the mainland 79
lost property 116
Lymington and around 98

M

maps 116
    Brighstone to Alum Bay 76
    Cowes 30
    Cowes and around 28
    Island Line 112
    Isle of Wight at a glance 8
    Newport 38
    Newport and around 36
    Ryde 46
    Ryde and around 45
    Sandown and Shanklin 58
    The east coast 50
    The south coast 57
    Ventnor to Blackgang 66
    Yarmouth 87
    Yarmouth and around 84
Meet Ferguson's Gang 86
money 116
Monkey HavenHaven 37
Mottistone Gardens & Estate 75
Museum of Island History 36

N

Needles Park 78
New Battery 79
New Forest, The 99
    camping 99
Newport and around 36
Newport Roman Villa 37

Newtown 85
Newtown National Nature Reserve 86
Newtown Old Town Hall 85
Northwood ParkPark 28

O

Old Battery 78
opening hours 116
Osborne House 29

P

Pirate's Cove & Jurassic Bay Adventure Golf 59
Portchester Castle 91
Portsmouth 91
    Charles Dickens' Birthplace 95
    HMS Victory 93
    HMS Warrior 93
    Mary Rose Museum 94
    National Museum of the Royal Navy 94
    Old Portsmouth 95
    Spinnaker Tower 93
    The Historic Dockyard 93
post offices 116
Priory Bay 51
public holidays 116
pubs
    Buddle Inn 73
    Castle Inn 43
    King Harry's Bar 63
    Pier View 35
    Red Lion 81
    The Anchor InnAnchor Inn 35
    The Bugle Coaching Inn 89
    The Compass BarCompass Bar 35
    The King's Head 89
    The Old Comical 63
    The Olde Village Inn 55
    The Old Fort 55
    The Pilot Boat Inn 55
    The Sun Inn 81
    The Taverners 73
    The Vectis Tavern 35
    The Volunteer 73
pubs (by area)
    Brighstone to Alum Bay 81
    Cowes and around 35
    Newport and around 43
    The east coast 55
    The south coast 63
    Ventnor to Blackgang 73
    Yarmouth and around 89

Q

Quarr Abbey 47

R

restaurants
    33 St Helens 54
    Ada Mediterranean Kitchen 48
    Fisherman's Cottage 61
    Folly Inn 33
    Ganders 54
    Gastronomy 33
    Heron 48
    Hewitt's 42
    Hungry Bear 54
    Le Tour du Monde 71
    Mojacs 33
    Murrays 33
    Off the Rails 88
    On the Rocks 88
    Prego 33
    Ristorante Michelangelo 49
    Salty's 89
    Smoking Lobster 70
    Spyglass Inn 70
    The Basque Kitchen 32
    The Best Dressed Crab 54
    The Bistro 70
    The Boathouse 54
    The Coast Bar & Dining Room 33
    The Duke of York 33
    The George 88
    The Hut 80
    The Red Duster 34
    The Smoking Lobster 34
    The Steamer Inn 62
    The Village Inn 62
    The Waterfront 80
    Thompson's 42
    Tonino's 34
    True Food Kitchen 71
restaurants (by area)
    Brighstone to Alum Bay 80
    Cowes and around 32
    Newport and around 42
    Ryde and around 48
    The east coast 54
    The south coast 61
    Ventnor to Blackgang 70
    Yarmouth and around 88
RNLI 53
Robin Hill Country Park 39
Round the Island Race 31
Ryde pier 44
Rylstone Gardens 60

S

Sandown 56
Sandown Pier 56
Seaview 50
Shanklin 59
Shanklin Chine 59
shopping 7

shops
  Alfie-in-the-Air 48
  Beachcomber 48
  Blue by the sea 88
  Blue Labelle 70
  Cavanagh & Baker 61
  Eclectica 32
  Medina Books 32
  Pencil Cottage 61
  Reflections 88
  Reggie's Retro 70
  Rosalie's of Cowes 32
  Slab 32
  The Rock Shop 61
  The Velvet Pig 48
  Ventnor Exchange 70
  Warren Farm 80
shops (by area)
  Brighstone to Alum Bay 80
  Cowes and around 32
  Ryde and around 48
  The south coast 61
  Ventnor to Blackgang 70
  Yarmouth and around 88
smoking 117
Southampton 97
  City Art Gallery 97

  The Sea City Museum 98
Southsea 96
  Blue Reef Aquarium 97
  D-Day Museum 96
  Southsea Castle 96
St Catherine's Oratory 69
St Catherine's Point 69
Steephill Cove 66
St Helens 53

T

Tapnell Farm 75
Tennyson Down 76
The Garlic Farm 38
The Isle of Wight Bus Museum 45
The Parade 27
the Romans 91
The Shipwreck Centre 38
The Sir Max Aitken Museum 26
The Wight Military and Heritage Museum 41
time 117
tipping 117
toilets 117
Totland 79

tourist information 117
trains 112
travelling to the Isle of Wight 110

V

Ventnor Beach 64
Ventnor Fringe Festival 65
Ventnor Heritage Centre 65

W

walking 113
walks from Niton 69
weather and climate 5
West Wight Alpacas and Llamas 84
Whippingham 31
Wildheart Animal Sanctuary 57

Y

Yarmouth and around 82
Yarmouth Castle 83
Yarmouth Pier 83

NOTES